SEA THE STARS

THE WORLD'S BEST RACEHORSE

SEA THE STARS

THE WORLD'S BEST RACEHORSE

ANNE HOLLAND

WEIDENFELD & NICOLSON

Contents

Chapter 1
A Model Racehorse

Sea The Stars

the very name has a magical ring. Horse of the season, the decade, the century – possibly of all time. The Arkle of the flat-racing world, he has captured the imagination of racing fans throughout Europe.

It is not just what he has won, but the manner in which he has done so: six Group Ones in six months, including the 2000 Guineas, the Derby and the Arc, the Big Three never before achieved by one horse in one season and only once anything approaching a close finish; all his wins were by convincing margins. If trouble appeared, he cast it aside with his scintillating speed, and he kept improving with every race. He held his own, and more, against older horses. Not for him the tag 'miler' or 'stayer', for he proved his superiority at three separate distances.

Sea The Stars is the model racehorse: handsome, even-tempered, intelligent. To have held him in his box, marvelled at his size, scope and demeanour, to have patted his neck and stroked his nose will for me remain one of life's privileges.

He is big, almost in the mould of a steeplechaser, with a magnificent frame overlaid with powerful muscles. On the move he has, like the very best athletes, great economy of effort, which makes him appear to

Pat Taafe rides Arkle to win the Cheltenham Gold Cup, 1965.

OPPOSITE: *Sea The Stars . . . relaxed, confident and charismatic . . .*

float over the ground. A beautiful bay with black points and no white on him, he is equine perfection. More than anything, his incredible temperament sets him apart. Most colts will be 'laddish' (testosterone is flowing in a three-year-old) and, trying to assert themselves, can bite and kick in the stable. Sea The Stars has an equanimity that has stood him in good stead when the pressure all around is at explosion point. If he can pass this, as well as his outstanding athleticism, on to his offspring, it will be a priceless asset.

Many a superstar has been undone by the electric atmosphere of Derby Day; many more have failed in the Arc because they have been unable to stay the course after so many high-profile races. In race after race, Sea the Stars bided his time and then appeared from nowhere, his exceptional acceleration and speed over the ground taking him well clear at the post.

The other ingredients required to bring out the best in a truly outstanding horse are also in place. Sea The Stars is blessed with a remarkable team: understanding, supportive owners, David and Ling Tsui and their son Christopher; his trainer, John Oxx, who is truly 'the gentleman of Irish racing', and his wife, Caitriona; and a jockey, Mick Kinane, who is quite simply at the top of his illustrious career. What's more, the successful Hong Kong owners notwithstanding, it is a triumphant Irish story at a time when that is sorely needed.

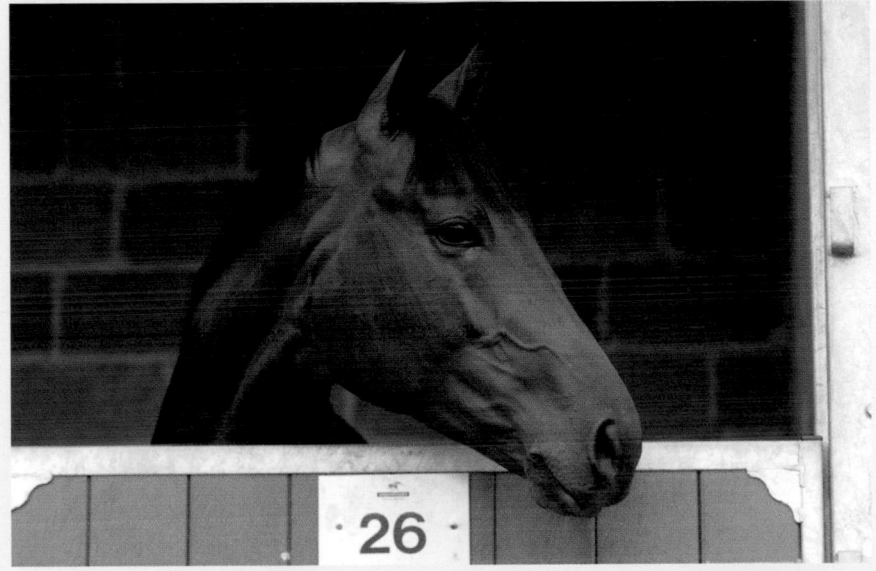

Chapter 2
Home Turf – The Curragh

The story of Sea The Stars

begins in Ireland, in particular in Kildare, the county where he was conceived, born, reared and trained and stands at stud. Often described as 'the thoroughbred county', Kildare boasts the Curragh racecourse, home to all five Irish Classics, as well as numerous famous and successful stud farms and training establishments.

The word 'curragh' itself means 'place of the running horse' and there are documented tales of third-century chariot races on this hallowed turf, which covers an area of about 5000 acres. By the early

OPPOSITE: *Early morning on the Curragh.*

LEFT: *Thoroughbreds exercising on the gallops, the Curragh.*

1700s, horse racing as we know it had been established in Kildare. More than a quarter of all racehorses in training in Ireland are based there, with over sixty trainers registered. Among them are Dermot Weld, Kevin Prendergast – and a certain John Oxx.

The Curragh and surrounding county boast some of the finest studs in Britain and Ireland. One such is owned by Sir Edmund and Lady Loder, who are only the second family of incumbents at Eyrefield Lodge in over a hundred years, following Henry Eyre Linde, trainer of consecutive Aintree Grand National winners Woodbrook and Empress in 1880–81. Sir Edmund's great-great-uncle, Major Eustace Loder, purchased Eyrefield Lodge in 1897 and bred one of the Turf's greatest fillies there, Pretty Polly. Described as looking 'almost too powerful', she won twenty-two of her twenty-four races, including, in a procession of brilliant victories, the fillies' Triple Crown of 1000 Guineas, the

ABOVE: *Sir Edmund Loder of Eyrefield Lodge whose ancestor bred the legendary Pretty Polly.*

BELOW: *Bernard Dillon on Pretty Polly c.1900 – winner of 22 of her 24 races.*

Oaks and the St Leger in 1904, as well as beating the leading colts of her generation in other races. She is the ancestor of many subsequent famous racehorses.

Sir Anthony and Lady O'Reilly, whose distinctive black and white colours are familiar on Irish racecourses and beyond, breed at Castlemartin Stud, Kilcullen, on the western edge of the Curragh.

If you drive south, once you have passed the Irish National Stud, the clipped hedges and neat rails of Kildangan Stud, where Sea The Stars was conceived, come into view. The Kildangan estate stretches for nearly 2000 acres from Kildangan village to Nurney. It was purchased by Edmund O'Reilly, from Dublin, in 1703 and his descendant Roderic More O'Ferall trained horses at Kildangan during the 1920s and 1930s before beginning a full-time breeding operation that became world renowned; eleven Classic winners were bred at Kildangan. Over five decades he established one of the finest studs in Ireland. Roderic died in 1990 aged eighty-seven, four years after selling the estate to Sheikh Mohammed bin Rashid al Maktoum, who has built it up into the headquarters of his seven Irish studs, the 3000-acre Celtic wing of his worldwide Darley thoroughbred empire.

Today Kildangan stands eight stallions, of which their flagship sire is Cape Cross, sire of Sea The Stars. The son of Green Desert won five

ABOVE: *Sir Anthony and Lady O'Reilly at the Independent Waterford Wedgwood Phoenix Stakes in 2002. Their Castlemartin Stud on the Curragh is a major breeding enterprise.*

LEFT: *Sheikh Mohammed bin Rashid al Maktoum at the St Leger Festival in 2003. He bought the Kildangan Stud over twenty years ago. Darley is now an eighteen-stud worldwide breeding enterprise.*

Cape Cross, Sea The Stars' sire, now stands at Kildangan Stud.

races (but lost one of those in the stewards' room) in a career spanning four seasons. He seemed to improve with age and won his only Group One at four years, smashing the course record in the process in the one-mile Lockinge Stakes at Newbury. He was Champion older miler at five when he won the Queen Anne Stakes at Royal Ascot and Goodwood's Celebration Mile, both Group Two.

Cape Cross's sire, Green Desert, stands only 15.2 hands high. His two wins at the age of two were over five furlongs and six furlongs, and his three wins at three years old included the Group One July Cup over six furlongs at Newmarket. He was also second to the great Dancing Brave in the 1986 2000 Guineas, over one mile. So it can be seen that Sea The Stars has sprinting blood – and small size – only two generations back.

Cape Cross was foaled and reared at Kildangan and it was fitting that he returned there after his racing career to stand at stud. Stud director Jimmy Hyland joined Kildangan in his twenties in 1987, a year after it was bought by Sheikh Mohammed. Jimmy has an impeccable pedigree for the job, having grown up barely a mile away at Oghill House Stud. He also gained experience at Treascon Stud, owned by his great-uncle Christy Mooney, home to stallions Aristocracy and Boreen, among others. Spells in Kentucky, Japan and at Thornton Hall in Yorkshire since he joined Darley have all added to his experience.

When I last visited, he showed me Cape Cross, drying off from his morning in the pouring rain, being groomed. All the stallions love a spell out at grass each day and they also have a session on the horse-walker, keeping them fit for the job of covering some of the finest mares. Cape Cross has himself sired one of the world's greatest mares, Ouija Board, early in his career.

Until 2009, Ouija Board was Cape Cross's star progeny; the bay mare, born in 2001, was as tough and as talented as they come, becoming a big favourite with racegoers. Owned by Lord Derby and trained by Ed Dunlop in Newmarket, she won the Oaks, the Irish Oaks, the Hong Kong Vase, the Breeders' Cup Fillies and Mares Turf twice and was third in the Arc. Her twenty-two-race career spanned four seasons and produced ten wins, seven of them at the highest Group One level, and eight places. Some of her races showed the utmost guts in the closest finishes.

It was because of this great mare in particular that the Tsui family chose Cape Cross for the next mating of their mare Urban Sea, and so,

ABOVE: *John Reid takes Cape Cross into a length-and-a-half win over Frankie Dettori on Josr Algarhoud in the Celebration Mile at Goodwood, August 1999.*

LEFT: *With Daragh O'Donoghue up winning the Juddmonte Lockinge Stakes at Newbury in 1998.*

Urban Sea, Sea The Stars' dam, ridden by Cash Asmussen to second place in the Prince of Wales Stakes, Royal Ascot, 1993.

in 2005, she came to be covered by Cape Cross, a mare who seemed to be able to produce winners from different types of stallions. John Clarke, then manager of the Irish National Stud where Urban Sea boarded, would draw up a shortlist and Christopher Tsui's mother, Ling Tsui, after discussing the options, would make the final decision. One of the factors influencing the choice of Cape Cross was that he had produced Ouija Board, and it helped that he also stood near by.

Ouija Board was an outstanding mare but Urban Sea, Sea The Stars' dam, will go down as one of the greats, in both racing and breeding. Urban Sea's dam was Allegretta, who initially seemed an unlikely brood-mare prospect, let alone one that would bear enormous influence in the early twenty-first century. Allegretta was born in Germany, by

Lombard, and traced back in the female line to a great foundation mare, Maid of Masham.

Despite her lineage, Allegretta herself proved to be of very dubious heart on the racetrack. After an initial promising second in the Oaks Trial, she got so wound up before the Oaks itself that she finished last. Then in the Park Hill Stakes, wearing blinkers, she virtually refused to race. It's hard to imagine this streak of temperament only two dams back from Sea The Stars. Sent to stud on the blue grass of Kentucky, Allegretta was barren in her first two years before producing four foals of limited talent, one of them providing a number of wins. She was consigned to the 1984 Keeneland November sale where, liking her looks and breeding while forgiving her temperament, Robert Nataf of Horse France purchased her for $55,000 on behalf of Michel Henochsberg's Marystead Farm. She was put in foal to Miswaki (USA), a son of a leading American sire, Mr Prospector. Miswaki raced in Europe and won the 1980 Grade 1 Prix de la Salamandre. A smart two-year-old, he passed on his speed to his offspring. Given the nature of Urban Sea's dam, Allegretta, it is interesting to note that Miswaki's dam was called Hopespringseternal! It was a mating that in January 1989 produced a chestnut filly who was to be named Urban Sea.

A year later, in 1990, Jean Lesbordes, a French trainer who had a small string for David Tsui, bought Urban Sea on behalf of David Tsui and partners for only 280,000 francs (£30,000) at the Deauville yearling

Pat Eddery on Placerville leads Urban Sea to the post in the Prince of Wales Stakes.

sales. Winner of a two-year-old maiden race in 1991, she ran eight times in France as a three-year-old, winning two, including a Listed race, and placing four times, including a Group One. Interestingly, on her second-ever run in France, she was ridden by one M.J. 'Mick' Kinane into third place. It was at the age of four, when again she ran eight times, that she improved even more, becoming a top-class filly at middle distances, culminating in victory in the 1993 Prix de l'Arc de Triomphe, at a price of 37–1, when she narrowly defeated White Muzzle, with Opera House and Intrepidity behind. Rated the best older mare in Europe at the age of four, she stayed in training at five when she added a Group Two win to her tally.

While she was good as a racehorse, it was at stud that Urban Sea excelled. Her first foal, the Bering colt Urban Ocean, won four races including a Group Three. Her second foal, Melikah, by Lammtarra (winner of the Derby, the King George and the Arc), was one of the very few worthwhile products of that lovely chestnut, wining the Pretty Polly Stakes, and finishing second in the English and Irish Oaks.

BELOW: *Urban Sea stunning the crowd at Longchamp winning the Arc in 1993 from White Muzzle and Open House, with Eric Saint-Martin (whose father Yves won the Arc four times) up.*

LEFT: *Galileo in training on the gallops.*

Four matings with Sadler's Wells followed with instant success: Galileo, born in 1998, won six of his eight starts, including the Epsom Derby, the Irish Derby and the King George VI and Queen Elizabeth Stakes. Since then he has rapidly established himself as a stallion – he was champion sire of 2008. Born a year later, Black Sam Bellamy was good without being as good as his illustrious brother. Nevertheless his four wins included the Group One Tattersalls Gold Cup and he stands at stud in Germany for a fee of just €6500. No doubt he will become more popular through his half-brother Sea The Stars, in addition to being the full brother to Galileo. Two progeny sired by Galileo include Teofilo and New Approach.

In 2001, Urban Sea bred a Giant's Causeway filly who was purchased for 1,800,000 guineas as a foal at Tattersalls Newmarket December sales, her half-brother Galileo having won the Derby et al. that summer. Named My Typhoon, she was sent to the USA and won six 'black-type' events, including the Group One Diana Stakes. Urban Sea then went to Green Desert, a match that produced Cherry Hinton who placed third in the Group Three Blue Wind Stakes.

It was in March 2005 that Cape Cross covered Urban Sea; the mating conceived the bay foal who was to be named Sea The Stars and on whom within a very few years the title Best in the World was to be bestowed.

BELOW: *Mick Kinane on Galileo celebrates after a three-and-a-half length win over Golan, the other joint favourite in the 2001 Epsom Derby.*

Chapter 3

The Irish National Stud
– A Star Is Born

Few flat-racing portents

appeared in the sky on Thursday, 6 April 2006. There was no racing in
Ireland. On the previous day, Gowran Park, and on the following day,
Wexford, were both National Hunt meetings. Ireland races on average
four or five days a week and more often than not these are mixed cards:
only Kilbeggan in County Westmeath is exclusively jumping, and the
Curragh has been joined by Dundalk's all-weather as flat-only tracks.

Across the water on that spring day there was a National Hunt meeting
at Taunton and an 'industry' card on the flat at Leicester, where even
the day's feature race paid less in prize money than in Ireland's lowest-
grade races. Most racing fans that day would have turned their attention
instead to the opening day of the Aintree Grand National Festival when
the feature, over part of the Grand National course, was the Liverpool
Foxhunters, won by the Waley-Cohens with Katarino. Two days later,
Numbersixvalverde was to be welcomed home to the Kildare stables of
Martin Brassil as hero of the Grand National.

But on that Thursday, in one of the large, straw-filled stables at the Irish
National Stud, a future star – Sea The Stars – was about to be born. The
seventeen-year-old mare Urban Sea was in labour: sweating, swinging her
head round to her flanks, lying down, getting up – restless. Having foaled
nine times before, she did not find it too difficult and moments after the

OPPOSITE: *A thoroughbred
mare and foal, the Irish
National Stud, Kildare*

birth began licking her foal. Still glistening wet, he looked nearly black but once he was dry, and standing on his long, wobbly legs, it was clear he was bay, like his half-brother Galileo. Could he emulate his brother in three years' time and win the Derby? Could he!

The Irish National Stud at Tully in County Kildare is one of Ireland's showcase tourist spots with much more than just horses on view. The only Irish stud open to the public, it hosts daily conducted tours between February and December where visitors may see the stallions – each of whom also has his own individual turn-out paddock for daily use – and the mares and foals. A number of mares are boarded there, Urban Sea having been one.

Visiting the stud on a sunny spring day is always a joy, with foals gambolling and plants coming to life in the Japanese Gardens; the Horse Racing Museum is well set out and has something to interest even non-horsey people. Lunch in the restaurant beside the gift shop can be walked off with a stroll by the lakeside Millennium Garden that commemorates the patron saint of gardeners, St Fiachra. Horse breeding is believed to have been an integral part of the area since about 1300, when it is thought that warhorses were bred for the

Knights of Malta. Tully itself was first set up as a stud farm in 1900, when the lands were purchased from a local farmer by Colonel William Hall-Walker, son of a former Mayor of Liverpool and scion of a rich Lancashire brewing family: his father had given Liverpool the Walker Art Gallery.

Four years before purchasing Tully, the colonel bought a horse called The Soarer prior to the 1896 Grand National. The low-weighted gelding promptly won it, in the hands of his vendor, Mr D.M.G. Campbell, later to become General Sir David Campbell. The Soarer, like many another winner in the 170-year history of the world's most famous steeplechase, fell the following year.

Colonel Walker set about turning his new farm at Tully into one of the best studs in Europe at the time, building up a collection of foundation mares that were to have tremendous influence on racing. In the ten-year period between 1904 and 1914, there were seven Classic winners bred at Tully, including Minoru who won the 1909 Derby and the 2000 Guineas in the colours of King Edward VII, Prince Palatine (winner of the St Leger and the Ascot Gold Cup) and Cherry Lass (winner of the Oaks and the 1000 Guineas).

ABOVE: *Part of the world-famous Japanese Gardens created at the beginning of the twentieth century.*

RIGHT: *A row of stalls at the Irish National Stud.*

ABOVE: *An aerial view of the extensive buildings of the Irish National Stud, the stallion boxes in the centre and the foaling yard above right.*

LEFT: *The grounds have been expertly landscaped and maintained over the sixty years of state ownership.*

On a boggy site near Tully House, he created a Japanese garden, which was laid out by eminent Japanese landscape gardener Tassa Eida and his sons Minoru (which means 'light of my eye' and after whom the Classic colt was named) and Kaiji, assisted by an army of local labourers. They worked on the project from 1906 to 1910. During that time the Eida family lived at Curragh House, which is now the Racing Apprentice Centre of Education, known as RACE. Tassa Eida died in 1912 on his intended return journey to Japan. No more was heard of him or his family until Brian Eida, a son of Minoru, turned up at Tully as a tourist in the late 1980s to admire the work of his grandfather Tassa.

In 1916, Colonel Hall-Walker, later Lord Wavertree, presented both Tully and his stud in Wiltshire to the British government for the purpose of founding a British National Stud, now located in Newmarket. The stud at Tully continued under the guidance of its first director, Sir Henry Greer, and bred top horses such as Blandford, Big Game and Sun Chariot.

In 1943, the Irish government took over the land and buildings at an agreed valuation. Two years later the Irish National Stud Company Ltd was formed and it officially took over the running of the stud on 31 August 1946. The gardens, which had fallen into neglect, were restored and, designed to symbolise the 'Life of Man', are now of international repute, acclaimed as the finest Japanese gardens in Europe.

The first Irish National Stud Thoroughbred Breeding Course was held in 1971. Every spring the course educates young people for a career in the breeding industry during the stud's busiest time of year, foaling and covering mares. It culminates in students taking oral and practical exams, leading to the recognised Irish National Stud Certificate. Many of its graduates have become managers at world-renowned studs or other captains of the racing and breeding industry.

Students are also taken from RACE, sometimes on a two-week trial. If they cope with mucking out and general helping without a saddle in sight and still love it – the smell, the atmosphere, the whole equine environment – then a career in racing will beckon.

The 900-acre stud continues to be owned by the Irish government and is run as a commercial enterprise under the chairmanship since 1988 of Chryss Goulandris, Lady O'Reilly. The stallions standing there in 2009 were Invincible Spirit, Celtic Swing, Elusive City, Rakti, Verglas, Indian Haven, Amadeus Wolf and Jeremy.

Chryss Goulandris, Lady O'Reilly, married former Irish International rugby star and industrialist Sir Anthony O'Reilly in 1991. A member of the board of the Irish National Stud since 1993, she has been chair since 1998. Here she talks to Pat Smullen after his victory in the 2009 Irish National Stud Blandford Stakes, at the Curragh racecourse.

The original ethos behind the Irish National Stud was to provide affordable stallions to cash-strapped Irish citizens. Today it is a self-financing business, making most of its money through the sale of stallion nominations (stud fees) worldwide. In addition, it keeps its own small band of brood mares whose progeny are sold annually. The tourism side also makes a profit, every penny of which, like the surplus from the nominations and the progeny sales, is ploughed back into the stud, making it a national asset to be proud of.

Although it is state-owned, the management has a free rein in making decisions. This was put to intelligent use at the end of 2008 when there was a catastrophic downturn in the thoroughbred breeding industry (along with most other aspects of Irish life amid the worldwide recession). The stud became the first to reduce its stallion fees, setting an example that was soon followed.

BELOW: *A mare and her colt, at the Irish National Stud.*

LEFT: *Urban Sea being beaten to the post, Royal Ascot, 1993.*

The chief executive for twenty-seven years was John Clarke, who had for some time also been bloodstock adviser to the Tsuis, who had bred Sea The Stars at the stud. He considered himself lucky to have been associated with such horses as Indian Ridge, Invincible Spirit, and Verglas prior to the stud having reared Sea The Stars.

Sadly, Urban Sea did not live to see the success of her mighty son. In early March 2009, aged twenty, she haemorrhaged after giving birth to a colt by Invincible Spirit, one of the stud's own stallions (by Green Desert). It was a melancholy day for the staff at Tully, as well as for the Tsui family. Urban Sea had lived there for eight years and was loved by one and all for her lovely nature, the trait she so successfully handed down to her son. She had beaten no less than fourteen Group One winners in the Arc. At the time of her death, seven of her eight foals to have raced had won Group races, including Classics on both sides of the Atlantic. Her greatness and legacy will live on down the generations.

Her death posed an immediate problem for the foal, who needed milk every couple of hours. Luckily a foster-mother was found in a half-bred grey mare by the name of Mini Pen; the pair bonded and the foal was successfully reared. On his head lies the chance of making his mother the only mare in history to produce three Derby winners . . .

From the start, Sea The Stars was big, weighing in at 142 pounds,

OPPOSITE: *Animal handler Hisanobu Minna leads a foal and her mare in from the paddocks at the Irish National Stud c.1994.*

RIGHT: *Sea The Stars was foaled at the Irish National Stud in 2006.*

while the average weight for a thoroughbred foal is 120 pounds. He combined size with strength and always possessed the style, charisma and confidence of a star – the qualities that mark him still. At about eight months he was weaned from his mother, probably the single most stressful event in a young equine's life. He would have been turned out

out to pasture with other foals and, as with schoolboys, begun playing games – galloping, cavorting, rearing and bucking in good spirits. Lessons had to be learned: to walk quietly on a head collar and lead rope no matter how keen he was to get out and gallop – or to come in for his feed; to have his feet attended to by the farrier; to take worm doses; and a year later breaking and hacking round an indoor school.

Not for him, however, the stress as a yearling of so many of his peers who would be going to the sales, to trot up and down in front of myriad spectators, to be handled and scrutinised. Sea The Stars was born with an owner for life, to run in their colours.

By the beginning of 2005, now officially a two-year-old, he was ready to go to his trainer. It was to be his good fortune that the youthful Sea The Stars was despatched to one of the true gentlemen of racing and took up residency in the Curraghbeg stables of John Oxx.

BELOW: Is that a kiss? Sea The Stars and his trainer, John Oxx.

Chapter 4

John Oxx – Training a Legend

'It couldn't happen

to a nicer person' or 'Everybody is so happy for John': to no one do those words apply more aptly than to John Oxx, to which I would only add the inclusion of his wife, Caitriona. He is revered throughout the tight-knit Irish racing world, where some people refer to John as Ireland's unpaid ambassador. Certainly, it would be hard to find anyone more

OPPOSITE: *John Oxx, with a wry smile.*

LEFT: *Giving directions on a morning exercise in winter at Curraghbeg.*

The great open spaces of the Curragh with thoroughbreds on their way to early morning exercise.

helpful, even in the midst of enormous pressure. John had previously had a Derby and an Arc winner (Sinndar, 2000), but in Sea The Stars he had possibly the best racehorse of all time. Throughout he has remained charming and approachable despite an innate shyness and modesty; above all, he has remained totally unruffled and unflappable, supported throughout by Caitriona.

Curraghbeg, or 'Little Curragh', where John Oxx grew up and where Sea The Stars was trained, lies at the south-western tip of the Curragh – the almost 5000-acre expanse of well-drained esker land that makes up the Curragh Plains of Kildare – within a stone's throw of Kildare town and surrounded by Kildare golf club.

The steeple of St Brigid's Cathedral in the town centre is clearly visible from the stables. St Brigid founded her convent in the late fifth century by the oak on the hill – Drum Criadh (ridge of clay), later renamed Cill Dara (the church of the oak) – and she is the town's patron saint. If you look straight ahead from Curraghbeg, through gaps in the pines that line the fairways, along the gallops and across the Dublin–Cork railway line, the Curragh racecourse is clearly visible. This is the course that the young John and his older sister Marie were taken to in 1962 when their father, also named John, had high hopes of success in the Irish

Derby with Arctic Storm, the 20–1 winner of the 2000 Guineas. Brother and sister took up their place early on the rails by the winning post to be sure of a good view.

The Derby, sponsored for the first time by the Irish Hospitals Sweepstake, was the second race and Arctic Storm, ridden by Bill Williamson, had the outside draw; he had to thread his way through the runners and failed by a short head to catch Tambourine II. It was the most exciting day of young John's life and from that moment he was hooked; one day, he would be a trainer.

The 1960s were a golden age in Irish racing, with Arkle and Tom Dreaper heading the National Hunt sphere, while on the flat both P.J. Prendergast and Vincent O'Brien sent enough winners over the water to lead their UK colleagues. In Ireland there was a strong contingent of American owners, their horses spread among trainers large and small.

John Oxx Senior began training privately in 1943 and in his very first season he trained a Classic winner, Solferino, in the Irish St Leger.

BELOW: *The golden age of Irish racing: Pat Taafe on his way to winning the Gallagher Gold Cup at Sandown on Arkle by twenty lengths from Rondetto and Mill House and beating Mill House's course record by an astonishing 17 seconds. It was the last time the two great rivals raced each other.*

When he set out on the public trail in 1948, just a year after marrying Maisie Moriarty, he had only nine horses; it was in 1950, the year his son John was born, that he purchased Curraghbeg. Today, 100 horses are trained there. John senior earned a reputation for success with fillies and ten years after taking out his full licence he was leading trainer. Seven Classic winners in the 1960s came via Merrymate, Lynchris, Pampalina, Arctic Storm, Hibernia and Biscayne, by which time the young John was taking more and more interest.

It was in 1979 that the current John Oxx took over the licence, having been his father's assistant since 1973, the year he graduated as a veterinary surgeon from University College, Dublin, where he met, and a year later married, Caitriona O'Sullivan.

The training got off to a shaky start at first, see-sawing between good and bad years when the virus was about, but John's first winner, Orchestra, also became his first Group winner that same summer of 1979. His first really good year was 1986, with a number of winners. Things took off from there so that, as at May 2009, he had secured thirty Group One winners to which total Sea the Stars has added a further five. That new total includes eleven Classic winners (meaning he has now overtaken his father).

'It's a pleasure training good horses,' he says, 'but the most important thing is to train for nice people. I'd rather train a lesser horse for a nice person than the other way round – but luckily we have had very, very few tricky customers over the years. I forget the bad moments and don't dwell on them. My first Classic win, in 1987, was a big moment: a three-year-old filly, Eurobird, won the Irish St Leger and it was the year my father died. She was owned by Mr and Mrs Gerald Jennings, who nine years earlier had had the Irish Oaks taken off their filly Sorbus. It was very controversial, for minor interference, and was the darkest day, so Eurobird's win was some sort of justice. It was also a breakthrough, coming at the right time for us. We were sent yearlings belonging to the Aga Khan in the autumn of 1988, so the business was growing.'

Two years later, he won the Irish St Leger again, this time with Petite Ile, but it was in 1995 that he achieved arguably his biggest breakthrough with the great mare Ridgewood Pearl. This strapping chestnut won an incredible quartet of top races in different countries that year: the Irish 1000 Guineas, the Coronation Stakes at Royal Ascot, the Prix du

ABOVE: *Out on the Curragh: John Oxx supervises his string.*

Moulin at Longchamp, and the Breeders' Cup Mile in Belmont, USA. Truly world class, Ridgewood Pearl is remembered by a bronze statue outside the main entrance to the Curragh racecourse.

Her local owners, the Coughlans – Sean from Kildare and Anne from Naas – had met in London where Sean had a number of jobs before settling on construction. As a boy, he used to go racing on Irish Derby Day by walking to the far side of the Curragh where it was open and free to all. He would peer through the railings to see the likes of the McGraths and the McCalmonts in their finery, and dream his dream of one day owning a horse good enough to be there.

When Sean Coughlan did start owning, he enjoyed beginner's luck: with the filly Ben's Pearl, who won the 1988 Irish Cambridgeshire. She retired to stud and produced first Ridgewood Ben who won the Gladness Stakes and then, returning to the stallion Indian Ridge, she foaled the mighty Ridgewood Pearl.

John Oxx recalls her as 'a cracking filly, big and strong, almost masculine, with a deep girth. She was a powerful galloper, as tough as a colt, and a filly apart to look at. She was owned by a super couple in the Coughlans.'

Continuing his tradition with fillies, John Oxx won the Irish Oaks for two years running: with Ebadiyla in 1997 and Winona in 1998. But it was the new millennium that saw a major breakthrough for this modest gentleman, who is respected throughout the industry. This time it was with a colt, Sinndar, belonging to the Aga Khan. The bay, by Grand Lodge, won the Epsom and Irish Derbys in 2000, as well as the Prix de l'Arc de Triomphe, the only horse ever to have recorded this fantastic triple achievement. Little could John have dreamed that an even greater treble lay nine years ahead, for what makes Sea The Stars' achievement unique is that he had the speed to win the Guineas over one mile, the stamina and balance to win the Derby and the durability to take in the Arc, too.

ABOVE: *Ridgewood Pearl with Johnny Murtagh up and trained by John Oxx wins the Breeders' Cup Mile at Belmont Park, New York 1995.*

'To win the Epsom Derby is every trainer's dream come true,' says John.

The race took place on 10 June 2000, the day after their daughter Aoife's twenty-first birthday, so they took her with them as a birthday treat. Three horses were ahead of Sinndar in the betting but his claims were solid (he was beaten only once in his career and that was by a head). As the race unfolded, Sakhee skipped clear and only Sinndar, ridden as

OVERLEAF: *Derby Day 2009, John Oxx is congratulated after Sea The Stars becomes the first horse for twenty years to complete the 2000 Guineas/Derby double. Mick Kinane and Sea The Stars look on.*

BELOW: *The Irish Derby, 2000, Johnny Murtagh and Sinndar sprint away to win by nine lengths over Glyndebourne. It is a Derby double – Sinndar had beaten Sakhee by a length at Epsom.*

ABOVE: *Johnny Murtagh and John Oxx lift the trophy for the Budweiser Irish Derby won by Sinndar at the Curragh, July 2000.*

always by Johnny Murtagh, could go with him. Up in the stands, Caitriona Oxx was having difficulty seeing the race because of the number of large hats blocking her view. 'But I could hear them getting nearer and could see the finishing line and I sensed it was him coming.'

Following Sinndar's win, their day was not over yet. After John had been interviewed by the press, he, Caitriona and Aoife were escorted to the royal box where they were presented to the Queen Mother. It was less than two months before her one hundredth birthday, 'but,' says John, 'she stood the whole time. She was keen to have a chat, was fascinated, and left us feeling she really did want to meet us.'

At last they got back to the car. 'We must have been sitting in it for fifteen minutes before any of us said a word. We were just so stunned, and full of emotion and disbelief,' John remembers. In 2009 it would be the Queen herself whom the couple met in the royal box.

A month after Sinndar's Derby win, amid much secrecy and subterfuge, Caitriona managed to have a portrait painted of Sinndar for John's fiftieth birthday.

Next was the Irish Derby and another emotional day. Could they win the race so narrowly denied to John Oxx senior with Arctic Storm? The answer was an emphatic, nine-length 'yes'.

And so to France for the Arc, the crème de la crème.

'We hardly dared hope, afraid we'd used up our luck,' says John. 'But Johnny Murtagh was bubbling with confidence; he's a great man for the big occasion. It was a perfect day, with beautiful weather. Not only had we had a winner there the previous day but earlier in the day our sprinter, Namid, bolted in for Lady Clague, our longest-established client. Sinndar's win was the icing on the cake.'

Since then John's run of success with colts has continued. In 2003, Alamshar, owned, like Ebadiyla and Sinndar, by the Aga Khan, won the Irish Derby. Dalakhani was the star three-year-old of that year and this was the only time he was beaten. He too was owned and bred by the Aga Khan but for stud purposes it was considered more important for Dalakhani's career to try to win the Irish Derby.

'However, in my report to His Highness after the Epsom Derby, I had said we felt Alamshar ran a bit green in that race and should improve. I felt he deserved to take his chance in the Irish Derby, and His Highness sportingly agreed.'

The race itself produced one of the great racing duels of that summer with the Aga Khan's two horses having the race to themselves up the straight, battling neck and neck all the way.

'His Highness ran to greet him in, as proud as punch. I think he felt Irish that day because there were so many cheers,' John remembers. 'He loves racing as a sport and a hobby and he understands it; he won't run a horse just for the sake of it.'

The following month, in convincing style, Alamshar won the King George and Queen Elizabeth Stakes at Royal Ascot, where the three-year-olds take on older horses.

Azamour was a more than worthy successor to Alamshar and was a favourite of John's, though it is hard to believe he did not win a Classic. Instead he added the St James's Palace Stakes and the Irish Champion Stakes to the Oxx roll of honour in 2004, and the Prince of Wales Stakes and another King George to his tally in 2005.

In 2006, Kastoria, owned like Azamour by the Aga Khan, added

BELOW: *The Aga Khan (owner) and The Queen congratulate John Oxx after Azamour's victory in the 2005 King George Stakes held at Newbury. It was Mick Kinane's fifth victory making him the most successful jockey of all time in the King George Stakes.*

another Irish St Leger to the roll.

John Oxx has put a lot back into Irish racing as a talented administrator. He was chairman of the Irish National Stud from 1985 to 1990; and of the Irish Racehorse Trainers' Association from 1986 to 1991, and from 1993 to 1996; and has been a member of or on the committee of a number of other influential organisations including RACE, the Racing Academy and Centre of Education, of which he is currently its conscientious chairman. In 2008 he was honoured with the Irish Racehorse Trainers' Association Hall of Fame award, and he has been the recipient of a number of other awards over the years.

Doubtless there will be numerous new ones to come at the end of 2009.

One of the aspects for which the Oxxes, both father and son, are well known is that Curraghbeg is not a betting stable; it means every horse runs on its merit every time – and can sometimes ensure a long price. Sea The Stars, about whom no doubt they were quietly hopeful before the 2000 Guineas, was sent off at 8–1, with no less than five of his fourteen rivals ahead of him in the betting.

Recalling memories of his father for the *Guardian* in September 2009, John spoke of his own good fortune that Sea The Stars walked into his life: 'My father was a great dreamer. I would have always hoped as a youngster to have really good horses. That means more to a trainer – to have a star horse, rather than a load of winners. It certainly means more to me. I was always reading about racing and great horses of the past. So when you grow up with the history of racing and the history of breeding the landmark horses that come along over a century and more,

ABOVE: *John Oxx speaking to journalists invited to a celebration event with Sea The Stars (below) at the Curraghbeg yard.*

BELOW: *Sea The Stars with John Oxx, groom John Hynes, and John's wife Caitriona at Curraghbeg.*

OPPOSITE: *Sea The Stars in the same box once used by Sinndar.*

to train one that's in that league gives you the greatest satisfaction.

'It's what you've worked for all your life and not something you can expect to get. It's a miracle really. You can work and work away, but these horses have to walk through your gate, don't they? You don't make them. It's just by chance they come along, and when they do you want to do them justice.'

John Oxx has certainly done justice to Sea The Stars.

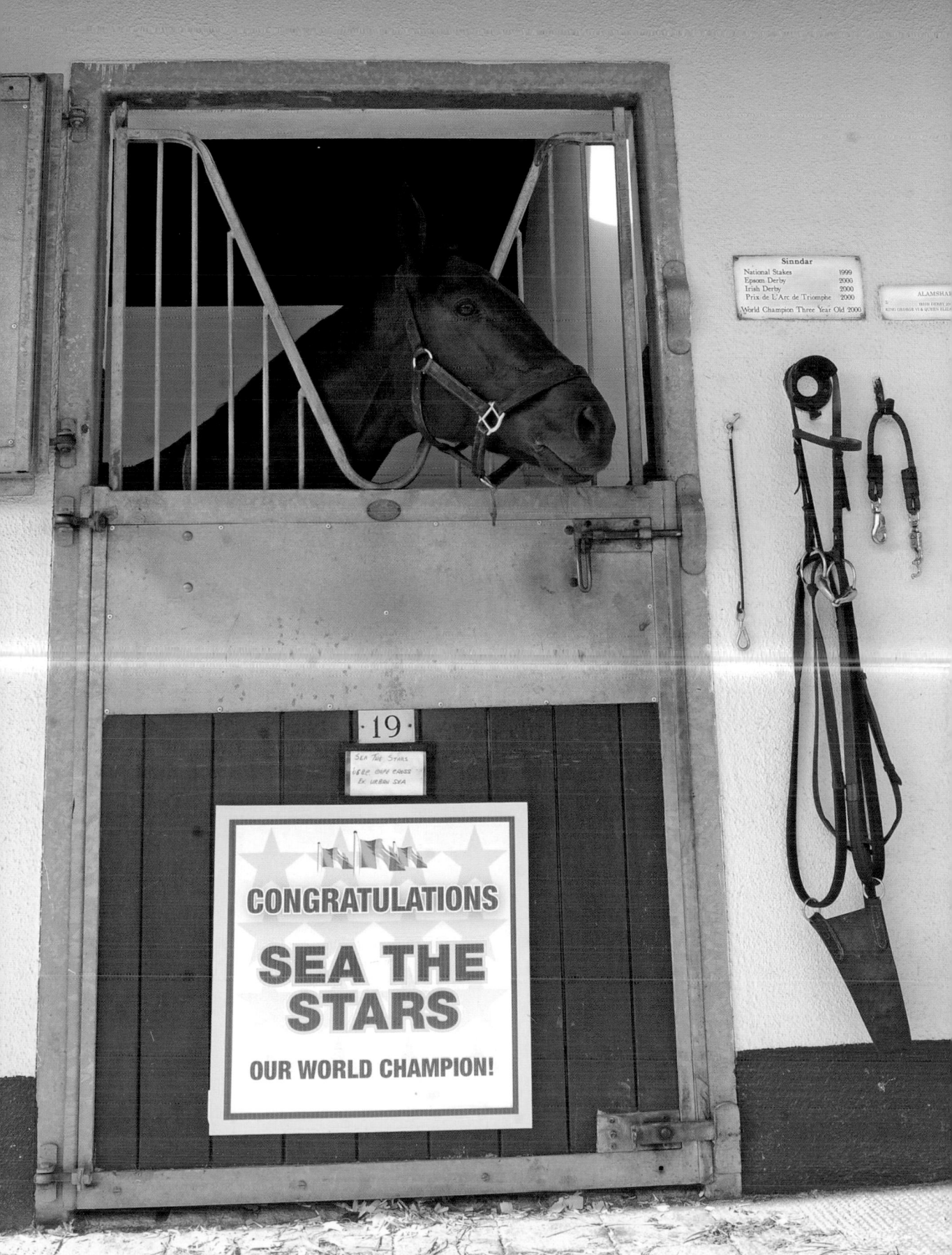

Chapter 5

Mick Kinane – Riding a Legend

Cheltenham, 15 March 1978.

Prestbury racecourse looks a picture beneath Cleeve Hill. National Hunt enthusiasts have flocked in their thousands to the first day of the Cheltenham Festival when the feature race is the Champion Hurdle. The ground is perfect and the prospect delectable.

Can Night Nurse, a big, almost lanky horse, join the elite band of horses to win the world's most coveted hurdle race for three successive years? He has an older pretender in Sea Pigeon to contend with, and a younger one, the compact, gutsy Monksfield, second to the champion the previous year and then dead-heating with him at Liverpool. Monksfield is ridden by a veteran jockey with a pugnacious determination and redoubtable ability, one Tommy Kinane.

There were ten other runners, too, making up the numbers. Coming to the last flight, Monksfield had seen off Night Nurse but now Sea Pigeon, ridden by Jonjo O'Neill, was coming at him. 'Monkey' skips away from the last and attacks the infamous hill as if his middle-aged jockey had set a blowtorch under him before going on to win. His second son, Michael, destined to become an even more famous jockey than his father, had won an apprentice race on Monksfield at Naas in April 1977.

Tommy Kinane grew up in rural Tipperary in a small house with his parents and his thirteen siblings, on an acre of land that provided

OPPOSITE: *Mick Kinane after winning the 2009 Epsom Derby. All the jockeys wore black armbands in memory of Vincent O'Brien, the trainer of six Derby winners, who had died that week at the age of 92.*

ABOVE: *Mick's father Tommy Kinane winning the 1978 Champion Hurdle, Cheltenham.*

sustenance for them all. Seven of the sons became involved in racing; Tommy started off with Tim Hyde and when he eventually retired from racing (he won six races on Monksfield and placed twelve times, but was controversially replaced before Monksfield won his second Champion Hurdle), he bought a ninety-acre farm and rented another hundred acres in County Tipperary. There he combined farming with training a small string of horses and with his wife Frances brought up their children.

Today, Tommy, now widowed, lives in a bungalow that stands sentinel at the top of a long, sloping, gravelled drive, leading down to the spacious, purpose-built house, barely a stone's throw from Punchestown that is home to his best-known son, Michael, his wife Catherine, and their two daughters. Tommy, an active member of the Irish Racegoers Club, went to Paris two weeks after the Arc with thirty or so others for the jumping at Auteuil and the flat at Longchamp. If he is riding on such occasions, Mick will usually join the party for lunch and, quietly but with a smile, give tips and sign autographs.

The large post-and-railed paddocks at Mick's home are grazed by mares and foals, progeny of some of the best horses he has ever ridden. The back drive is even longer; yearlings in the field beside it often come galloping up inquisitively. At the bottom is his stable barn and outdoor ménage, home to his budding breeding enterprise and to some of his ebullient brother Paul's hunters. It was here that Mick bred Authorised, winner of the 2007 Derby, a son of Montjeu on whom Mick won the King George VI and Queen Elizabeth Stakes at Royal Ascot in 2000.

When he won the Champion Hurdle, Tommy was forty-five (much older than most of the 'jumping boys'), and Mick was two weeks away from his fiftieth birthday when he won his third Derby, riding Sea The Stars.

Being associated with such a horse is no coincidence, for Mick has been at the top of the Irish – and the international – tree for many years. He had won the Derby twice before, on Commander-In-Chief in 1993 and on Sea The Stars' half-brother Galileo in 2001.

Tommy Kinane, one of the leading National Hunt jockeys of his day.

BELOW: *Mick Kinane at starting gates used for training in the 1993 season.*

ABOVE: *Dermot Weld, qualified vet, ex-jockey and holder of the record for most winners trained in Ireland.*

BELOW: *Mick at home with his dog Fred, 2002.*

From learning to ride at home on his father's horses, Mick rode his first winner on Muscari in Leopardstown in 1975 and was Champion Apprentice of 1978 when attached to Liam Browne's successful Curragh stable. He also won his first Classic for Liam, himself a former Champion Apprentice, riding Dara Monarch to victory in the 1982 Irish 2000 Guineas.

He spent a couple of seasons with Michael Kauntze and from there moved to Dermot Weld, from where, in 1985, he became Champion Jockey for the first of thirteen times in Ireland, with – at the time – a record number of 105 winners in a season. Dermot, he feels, honed the rough edges and helped him become a world-class jockey. The job took him round the world, too, notably when the two became the first Europeans ever to win Australia's Melbourne Cup, with Michael Smurfit's Vintage Crop in 1993. They are also the first and, so far, the only Europeans to win a leg of America's Triple Crown, at the 1990 Belmont Stakes with Go and Go. He has also won four Breeders' Cup races in the States.

Michael Smurfit was unable to attend Vintage Crop's historic Melbourne Cup win but was there two years later when in defeat he believes he ran one of his best races for 'the incomparable Dermot Weld and the dynamic Mick Kinane'.

Since those days Mick has ridden big winners in numerous countries, including India, Canada, Saudi Arabia and Slovakia; in the better-known world centres like Hong Kong, Japan, and the United Arab Emirates; and, closer to home, in Germany, Italy and France, as well as, of course, in the UK where he has ridden numerous Classic winners: the 2000 Guineas four times, the Derby three times, the Oaks twice and the St Leger once.

Many of these races came after his time with Dermot, when he was retained by Coolmore for Aidan O'Brien's Ballydoyle string, the biggest and probably the most advanced of its kind in Ireland. His mounts included Rock of Gibraltar, High Chaparral, Giant's Causeway and Galileo, Hawk Wing, Johannesburg and Montjeu, not to mention many more familiar names on the world racing stage.

ABOVE: *Sir Michael Smurfit, industrialist, philanthropist and owner of Vintage Crop, winner of the Melbourne Cup in 1993.*

LEFT: *Mick Kinane on High Chaparral with trainer Aidan O'Brien (right).*

Matters changed in 2004 when Mick found himself heading for the quieter waters of Curraghbeg. Perhaps its more 'homely' set-up suited him and his need for personal involvement: to be 'making' young horses, sorting through the two-year-olds, picking out the likely future winners – and, in one case, the special one. He felt at home and he loved it.

Life is full of twists and turns of fate, nowhere more so than in racing, which is a true leveller. In the jumping game, in particular, one jockey's injury can turn into another's good fortune; it can also happen in flat racing. Johnny Murtagh could so easily have been the man on board Sea The Stars but for an injury. He had originally worked for John Oxx as an apprentice from RACE, quickly rising to Champion Apprentice. With experience under his belt he became stable jockey to John Oxx for a fruitful eighteen years, culminating in 2003 with victory on John Oxx's Alamshar in the Irish Derby. Towards the end of that season a horse reared over him in the stalls and he cracked his coccyx. It caused was on the sidelines he gained weight. During the winter he could not in all sincerity tell John Oxx whether or not he would recover in time for the 2004 season. During that period of uncertainty, Mick Kinane became available and so, with no hard feelings, Johnny lost his retainer. (However, in the absence of Kieren Fallon, Johnny has gone on to ride outstanding winners for Coolmore.) Thus Mick Kinane's destiny with Sea The Stars was forged.

He might have had equals, but no one could have ridden Sea The Stars better, in all nine of his races. The 2008 season was the first time since the mid-1980s that Mick Kinane had not ridden a Group One winner; to an outsider it might have appeared time to quit, to call an honourable retirement. But Mick knew there was one horse waiting in the wings, potentially so special that, far from sailing off into the sunset, he spent the winter months pounding the sunlit streets of Dubai, five miles at a stretch. Nine months and six consecutive Group One wins later, amid the hectic scenes surrounding the announcement of Sea The Stars' retirement, Mick and his wife Catherine took themselves off for a couple of days to the tranquillity of the River Shannon, all question, for the moment, of his own retirement forgotten.

Mick Kinane gives Sea The Stars a well-deserved pat after the 2000 Guineas (above) and the Arc (left).

Chapter 6

Christopher Tsui – Owning a Legend

Christopher Tsui was a boy

of about ten when his parents' mare, Urban Sea, won the Prix de l'Arc de Triomphe at Longchamp in 1993. The exhilarating victory, coupled with the excitement, glamour and atmosphere of Longchamp on Arc day, made a lasting impression on him. As he went to school in Paris, it was not long before he was making weekend visits to the mare at the stables of trainer Jean Lesbordes. It was he who taught Christopher to ride. Soon he was going racing whenever Urban Sea ran, usually deputising for his mother who then, as now, preferred to stay away, working in the background. The mare became an integral part of his young life, almost like a member of the family.

In the end it was a different sport – golf – that pulled Christopher away. A professional career looked likely after he graduated from the David Leadbetter Academy in Orlando. He played on a few PGA tours including one in Canada, but found the golf course was not the place for him. Christopher returned to university, attending the Cass Business School in London. His parents, doubtless remembering how much as a boy he had enjoyed watching Urban Sea, lured him back to racing by giving him the colt they were keeping, Sea The Stars.

When Christopher graduated with his MBA in 2008, he not only became involved in his parents' businesses – mainly real estate, hotels

ABOVE: *Christopher Tsui with his lucky red tie.*

OPPOSITE: *Leading Sea The Stars, the winner of the Epsom Derby, with groom John Hynes.*

ABOVE: *Urban Sea, Sea The Stars' dam, surges through to win the Arc at Longchamp.*

RIGHT: *Galileo, Sea The Stars' sire, wins the Derby with Mick Kinane, Epsom, 2001.*

and international trading – but he also rediscovered the excitement of racing through his two-year-old – and how!

His mother is also adviser to Sun Jiadong, Chinese former vice-minister of aerospace and the chief architect of China's lunar exploration programme. Ling Tsui is known as a leader with a razor-sharp brain and as an astute businesswoman who makes her own decisions. However, with their horses she is more inclined to follow gut feeling than statistics, however persuasive the figures might look. Like many breeders, the Tsuis had sold Urban Sea's progeny but, with the mare getting older, they decided to keep the Cape Cross colt. One Derby winner, Galileo, had been part of a foal share with Coolmore although their share was sold before he ever ran. Perhaps this latest colt could give them a second chance of owning a Derby winner . . .

At the time of Urban Sea's retirement to stud, the Tsuis had a band of about forty brood mares, mostly in France, but they knew Ireland was where they wanted their star mare to be based for breeding. Over the following years, on the advice of the late Brian Grassick, they steadily reduced the numbers of their less good mares and replaced them only with a few good quality Irish fillies. When possible they liked to use King's Best, a half-brother to Urban Sea, and Galileo as sires.

When Urban Sea was at the Irish National Stud, the stud's chief executive John Clarke was a knowledgeable adviser. Nevertheless, intuition still came into it; other stallions were considered for Urban Sea in 2008 but Mrs Tsui had been so impressed by Ouija Board, both as a racehorse and for her personality, that she plumped for her sire, Cape Cross.

By the time of Urban Sea's death in early 2009, they had five mares, including Epping, dam of a winner, Dress Rehearsal, and Sassenach, who produced The Last Drop, runner-up in the St Leger, both of them by Galileo. They also had one other horse in training, a two-year-old brother to The Last Drop called Nebula Storm. Eight days after the Arc, the colt made his debut for the John Oxx, Michael Kinane and Christopher Tsui combination in a maiden at the Curragh, finishing in mid-field behind the odds-on Aidan O'Brien favourite, Midas Touch.

With Sea The Stars now to stand at stud at the Aga Khan's Gilltown, and Christopher home from university, it is hoped he will take a hands-on role in the breeding project and acquire mares suitable for their

ABOVE: *Christopher Tsui and Sea The Stars. '. . . we had many expectations for him from the start . . .'.*

superstar. It's a project that has perhaps been dormant in him since his schoolboy racing dates with Urban Sea, the mare who did so much for the Tsuis. From three runs as a two-year-old, Urban Sea won a maiden, but from thereon, from three to five years, she never ran in anything less than a Listed race. She finished second in the German 1000 Guineas at Düsseldorf, ridden just that once by Mick Kinane (finishing fast from the rear to be beaten by only a quarter of a length). Two wins and two more places in France saw her line up for the Rothmans International at Woodbine, Canada, in October, where she was second, beaten by half a length by Snurge.

At four she came straight into form, winning the Group 3 Prix Exbury before travelling to Sha Tin, where she was unplaced in the Hong Kong Cup. Royal Ascot saw her run second in the Prince of Wales Stakes, followed by three wins in a row in France, culminating in her neck victory over White Muzzle in the Arc. As a result she was invited to

Tokyo to take part in the Japan Cup, run at the end of November, but she was unplaced. The following April, by which time she was five years old, saw her win first time out again, followed by a third in the Group One Prix Ganay and fourth in the Coronation Cup at Royal Ascot. After this, a fetlock injury ended her career, one that was uncannily like All Along's whose box by chance she occupied.

Throughout her racing career, Urban Sea ran in the name of Hong Kong businessman David Tsui. When it was time to put her in foal, the Tsuis were happy to take the advice that Ireland was the best place to be, eventually moving from the Coolmore operation to the Irish National Stud. She was booked in to return to Cape Cross in 2009; sadly, with her loss there will never be a full brother or sister to Sea The Stars – but then perhaps he is unique anyway.

After the death of Urban Sea, Christopher Tsui told the press, 'My mother learned all about racing and breeding with Urban Sea. She followed her racing and breeding career step by step and she was devastated when Urban Sea died in March. Sea The Stars was always very relaxed and had a great temperament, just like his mother.

BELOW: John Oxx congratulates Mick Kinane after the 2009 Epsom Derby. John Hynes (second left) and Christopher Tsui walk alongside.

We had many expectations for him from the start, and I believed he would become great . . .'

After Sea The Stars' victory in the Derby, when Christopher was invited up to the royal box, he said, 'The occasion was so grand, I could feel the history as I was walking around Epsom Downs. To meet the Queen after the race was also a wonderful experience for me, something I will remember for a long time.'

Returning to his love for racing and his feelings for Sea The Stars in particular, he said, 'It is always tough for everybody when a great racehorse goes to stud, but it is much harder when he is the world's greatest horse. I and all those connected with him will feel empty after such an exciting and memorable year. I think 2009 will be a highlight of my life, and when I am eighty years old, I will still be talking about each victory of Sea The Stars to my grandchildren . . . Although his racing career has been very exciting, we are also looking forward to his stud career, as I am very interested in the breeding side of things. Urban Sea was the greatest brood mare ever, and to carry on her legacy is something I will be working on keenly with my team.'

RIGHT: *Some of the spoils of the season: (above left) The Coral Eclipse, Sandown, July 2009, (above right) The Juddmonte International Stakes, York, August 2009 and (below) the Derby, Epsom, June 2009.*

BELOW: *The closing stages of the 2009 Arc. Sea The Stars has threaded his way through the runners and is beginning to move ahead of the pack.*

Chapter 7

2008 – First Races as a Two-Year-Old

One of the aspects of riding

for John Oxx that Mick Kinane enjoys most is sizing up the newly broken two-year-olds. As both men are quiet by nature, neither is inclined to jump up and down in excitement at any particular prospect. However, both recall one morning in April 2008 when John pointed to a big bright bay two-year-old and asked Mick to ride him. Curious, Mick asked who it was.

A half-brother to Galileo, came the reply. As Mick had ridden Galileo to victory in the Derby, the Irish Derby and the King George – but for Aidan O'Brien, not John Oxx – he was now intrigued. Once he had returned from the canter, he was impressed. From that day on, when it came to 'fast work', Mick was on the youngster called Sea The Stars.

A jockey does much more than just sit on top of a horse. In a race he needs to be as physically fit as any athlete, with strong arms, legs, buttocks, and good lungs; above all he must have a clear head and a 'racing brain'. Some of the best jockeys are born, while others are made. Jockeyship is an art that has very little to do with brute force and much to do with empathy and skill. When it comes to young horses, before they even see a racecourse the man or woman on top has a crucial job to perform, in nursing, nurturing and teaching, allowing the youngsters to learn at their own pace. Just like children, some horses are sharper than others and will cotton on more quickly, but slow learners can end up being just as good, given time and patience.

The first time on a racecourse is equally crucial. Give a horse a hard time or a bad experience and it may be scarred for life; whipping it to win may ensure that it never wins again. Some jockeys are specialists in this nursery field, handing over later to the bigger stars when their charges are ready for the premier-league races.

Big is not always better in a horse; like a child it can 'outgrow its strength'. Sea The Stars was both big and strong. Out on the gallops, as the workload increased and the youngsters progressed, it was the big colt who was moving fast, as one born to it, a natural. Mick found Sea The Stars an easier ride than Galileo. It soon became apparent that he had a high cruising speed, smooth change of gear and excellent acceleration. A Ferrari among the Fords, but his temperament was sheer Rolls-Royce – and that was what set him apart.

Mick was to say later that although he had ridden some very good horses, Sea The Stars was the only one he believed capable of winning both a 2000 Guineas and a Derby. It is surprising to the layman, perhaps, just how much difference half a mile can make in a racehorse: the Guineas is for the speedsters, sprinters who are unlikely to have the stamina for the Derby, while the Derby prospects, bred to stay, are unlikely to have the fleetness of foot for the Guineas.

Horses and riders on an early-morning workout on the Curragh, January 2008.

In the preceding four decades before 2009, only two horses had proved capable of the double: Nijinsky and Nashwan. A good many others tried and failed.

It was on 13 July 2008 that Sea The Stars was deemed ready to make his racecourse debut and a seven-furlong maiden race at the Curragh was chosen.

Eighteen runners lined up on the good, springy Curragh turf, barely a mile away from Sea The Stars' stable; a number of them had already run, which gave them the advantage of experience and possibly fitness. The favourite was Tomas An Tsioda for trainer Jim Bolger. He made most of the running for the first six furlongs, but coming into the closing stages the race lay between Driving Snow, Black Bear Island, Freemantle and Sea The Stars; they finished in that order just ahead of Tomas An Tsioda.

Driving Snow, sporting the black and white colours of Lady O'Reilly and trained by Kevin Prendergast, had run third on his previous

LEFT AND BELOW: *The closing stages of Sea The Stars' first race, The Jebel Ali Stakes Maiden, the Curragh, July 2008. Driving Snow wins, Sea The Stars is a close fourth.*

outing. In winning that day, he became the only horse ever to beat Sea The Stars, while the first three became the only horses ever to finish in front of him in a race.

They had varying success subsequently: Driving Snow ran twice more the following month, finishing third and fourth, and then moved to America where, for new trainer Darrin Miller, he was beaten by a head on his first run that October. He was put away for the winter and notched another win first time out in July 2009 but was then injured.

ABOVE: *Sea The Stars with his groom John Hynes.*

BELOW: *First win: the Korean Racing Authority European Breeders' Fund Maiden, Leopardstown, August 2008.*

Black Bear Island, by Sadler's Wells, trained by Aidan O'Brien, won next time out in Naas at long odds-on and was put away for the winter. In April 2009 he travelled first to Longchamp for a Group Three race in which he finished third and then to York for the Group Two Dante Stakes as his prelude for the Derby, in which he finished tenth of the twelve runners behind Sea The Stars. More travel followed with another trip to Longchamp, unplaced, and finally a head second in the Group One Secretariat Stakes, Arlington. So the horse that had once finished ahead of Sea The Stars reached the end of 2009 with total earnings of £274,445; by comparison, his former victim notched up £4,417,163 . . .

Freemantle, by Galileo, and also trained by Aidan O'Brien, won a maiden at his third attempt. Then in 2009 he was beaten by a head by his stable companion, Black Bear Island, in York. He then finished fifth at Royal Ascot and fourth in the Group One Grand Prix de Paris in Longchamp. His total earnings: £77,319.

The three horses that beat Sea The Stars in his initial maiden race did so by a head, a neck and half a length, in other words by barely one length, and he had not been given a particularly hard time. He went home to a regular routine of feeding (he has always been an unfussy eater), grooming and training. His lad John Hynes – always smartly

Approaching the finish, Leopardstown, 2008. Despite heavy going, Sea The Stars finished comfortably ahead of the field.

turned out himself – groomed him until his coat shone.

Five weeks after his first run, with that wet August of 2008 having turned the ground soft-to-heavy, Sea The Stars' yellow colours with a purple star on a yellow cap duly passed the post first for the first time – in a maiden race at Leopardstown. Always prominent on the inside of the seven-furlong race, he went into the lead two furlongs out and stayed on well, putting two and a half lengths between himself and the nearest of his thirteen pursuers, headed by Dark Humour. Few spectators on the course that day realised they had just witnessed history in the making.

For his next race, the one-mile Group Two Juddmonte Beresford Stakes at the Curragh on 28 September, at almost the end of the season, was chosen to step up his racing experience. Just six runners lined up. Sea The Stars was not the favourite; instead, Aidan O'Brien's Masterofthehorse was sent off at 11–8 with Sea The Stars on 7–4. Aidan had two other runners; Kevin Prendergast had one, Recharge, and making up the field was another of John Oxx's called Mourayan.

PREVIOUS PAGES,
ABOVE AND RIGHT:
*The last race of 2008
and as a two-year-old,
the Juddmonte Beresford
Stakes, the Curragh in
September. Sea The Stars
moved clear in the last
fifty yards to win by half
a length from his stable
companion Mourayan.*

The ground was good that day and Mick Kinane tucked Sea The Stars in behind the leaders, moving up to fourth at halfway. As they came into the closing stages, it was a close-fought race. In the last fifty yards Sea The Stars stretched clear of the field, the next three finishing virtually in a line. His stable companion, Mourayan, finished a half-length behind in second, a short head in front of Masterofthehorse, with Recharge only a neck behind him. Mourayan went on to win a Listed race at the end of the 2008 season.

There were no more runs for Sea The Stars as a two-year-old. He had done what he had been asked to do that year and the feeling in Curraghbeg was that there could be considerably more in his locker for 2009. First, however, the debate began about the race distance most likely to suit his style of racing. Would he be a Derby horse like his half-brother Galileo, or might he have the speed for the 2000 Guineas, in which case he was unlikely to have the stamina for the Derby? Few people at that stage imagined him capable of both.

Mick Kinane had an inkling. He went off to Dubai with a spring in his step belying the fact that he was in his fiftieth year. A great camaraderie has built up among the racing fraternity, especially between the senior jockeys, since they began spending their winters out in the Gulf, soaking up the warmth, about twenty years ago; the standard of racing has kept on improving, too. Mick, a natural lightweight and about 5 feet 4 inches in height, embarked on his regime of five-mile runs and gym work, ensuring that there would be no one fitter the following summer. He had something very special to look forward to.

Chapter 8

May and June 2009 –
Two Classics

Mick Kinane was certain

that Sea The Stars was capable of winning both the 2000 Guineas and the Derby. 'He's laid back and yet wants to do the job. He is unique,' he told the press. John Oxx was less likely to say so, at least publicly, but got on quietly with the job of training the youngster, who had grown and matured, even seeming more eager than ever on his return to training after his winter rest.

The pedigree was there, of course. In training it became evident he had that perfect combination: a long stride coupled with an economical action and a robust constitution. Some horses are made nervous and excitable by new and strange experiences and refuse to feed. Sea The Stars by contrast had an entirely equable temperament and tucked into his fodder with gusto, regardless of any excitement – he never left an oat in his manger.

As he grew and progressed, it was evident that he thrived on work. If he was not worked hard enough, he was like a coiled spring waiting to explode into action. There was just one day in his career when Sea The Stars was off colour. On St Patrick's Day, 17 March 2009, he ran a temperature and had to be on the 'easy list' for a week. A trainer has

OPPOSITE: *The first race – and win – of 2009, the 2000 Guineas at Newmarket in May.*

a set work schedule building up to the big races and to miss a period of preparation can make the difference between victory and defeat. But within a week Sea The Stars was relishing his workouts again and continued to improve.

John Oxx was to say later, 'Whether he's done a hard day's work or not, he's the same. Those horses that have this toughness, this temperament, are set apart from the rest. He seems to be able to shake off ailments although he doesn't get them much to begin with. And he demolishes every feed. That's a terrific thing in a horse. You get only a small number who will eat like he does. He needs work. He needs to keep on the move if he's to keep settled and quiet in himself. He's a big strong athlete who likes to canter and likes to work. So you wouldn't give him a holiday anyway. You'd find it hard to give him a holiday. You'd find it hard to just trot him for three weeks. He'd be on springs.'

The 2000 Guineas was on 2 May and the talk beforehand centred on the Irish–English clash – but did not involve Sea The Stars. Brian Meehan's Delegator was the favourite ahead of Aidan O'Brien's Rip Van Winkle, Sir Michael Stoute's Evasive, and Jim Bolger's Gan Amhras. Sea The Stars, without a previous run that season, was not even a certain starter.

It was at about this time that I was trying to arrange a visit to John Oxx to talk about his father as well as himself and the various horses they had trained over the decades, for a book entitled *In The Blood*. Looking at John's diary with Caitriona was an eye-opener. That April morning, Caitriona searched around for a suitable date. John was in Limerick that day with runners and would be in Navan on Sunday with the Aga Khan's Alandi (who, with Mick Kinane up, would steamroller the mighty Yeats, trained by Aidan O'Brien. Yeats was to win a record-breaking fourth Ascot Gold Cup and retired after coming in third behind Alandi in the Prix du Cadran at Longchamp. Midweek John would fly to Newmarket to walk the course in advance of the 2000 Guineas. Come the weekend, he was due to be back there, if he had deemed the ground suitable, with his runner, a certain colt called Sea The Stars.

It remained John's conviction throughout that summer that Sea The Stars did not respond well to heavy ground. There was even a period when he said that if it stayed too wet to run him (and July and August were exceptionally soggy months), he might remain in training as a four-year-old. That is a key to John's success: nothing and no one will pressurise him into making a wrong decision. It is no coincidence that his Derby record is two winners and a third from three runners.

So he walked the course and prodded the ground – and was pleasantly surprised by its condition. It was going to be a fast race.

Newmarket and the Curragh are similar in that they are on well-drained, springy ground that dries out quickly – but if there is a deluge shortly before a meeting, even they will produce heavy ground. So John

ABOVE AND BELOW: *Winning in style, the 2009 2000 Guineas.*

ABOVE AND BELOW: *The final stages of the 2000 Guineas. Mick Kinane has detached Sea The Stars from the pack and is moving away from the frontrunners to win by a length and a half from Delegator, the favourite.*

flew back to Ireland and Plan A was put into action: Sea The Stars would take his chance in the 201st running of the Stan James-sponsored 2000 Guineas. Conversely, Arazan, his first string horse, would not run, as he likes – as John puts it – 'some ease'.

A few days later the principal players were in Newmarket. Sea The Stars' price could be found at 10–1 and he started at 8–1, with five of the fifteen runners at shorter prices. The manner in which Sea The Stars won the Guineas was an emotional rollercoaster. To begin with, three or four horses broke away, pulling hard. Delegator, the favourite, and Rip Van Winkle were held in near the back by their respective jockeys, Jamie Spencer and Kevin Manning, while Gan Amhras was closer to the front action. Mastercraftsman (Pat Smullen) and Sea The Stars

were also held up but remained in touch with the leaders. Both Aidan O'Brien's runners seemed to be short of room. As the field entered the final two furlongs, the result looked to lie between Delegator, Gan Amhras, Rip Van Winkle and Mastercraftsman. Sea The Stars was moving up smoothly, although these and other horses were ahead of him. Then, accelerating fast out of the pack in a style that he was to make his own, the horse in the yellow colours surged forward to gallop past his rivals to the post.

'It is horses like this that get you out of bed in the morning,' John told the press. 'He's a horse with a great future. He's got everything – speed, temperament, size, strength. He is a beautiful horse. He is such a presence in the yard and is such a pleasure to look at and train.'

For the record, the minor placings were Delegator, Gan Amhras, Rip Van Winkle and Mastercraftsman – but they, good horses in their own right, were relegated to being the supporting cast. Immediately after the race, Sea The Stars was installed as ante-post favourite for the Derby (although that did not remain the case) while his entourage returned to the Curragh to celebrate.

It was a few days later that I had my appointment with John Oxx. How lucky I was that there hadn't been time before the Guineas, for John was now able to show me his latest Classic winner with a touch of quiet pride. We walked into Sea The Stars' stable (it wouldn't be wise to do that with a great many colts), and the lad stripped off his rugs. His coat shone but above all it was the sheer size of him that impressed; not big as in gangly, or heavy, or unfurnished, but a shape and length more akin to a perfectly moulded steeplechaser. His conformation is faultless and from the way he 'stood over the ground' it was easy to see why he has such a lovely action with his long, ground-devouring stride. His demeanour was calm

BELOW: *Approaching the winning post, the 2009 2000 Guineas.*

ABOVE: *A congratulatory pat for Sea The Stars from Mick Kinane. John and Caitriona Oxx look on.*

LEFT: *Posing with the 2000 Guineas individual trophies.*

and his eye kind as he stood quietly while I patted his neck and stroked his nose, then stood back just to look at him again.

It was then that John smiled and, knowing my favourite winter pastime, said, 'I bet you wouldn't mind facing a fence on him out hunting.' We laughed, and I took hold of the head-collar rope and held him while his lad re-rugged him. I knew I had seen a magnificent specimen of a horse, but little guessed even then what lay in store . . .

One of the lovely characteristics of Sea The Stars is his way of going. So many photographs show him with his leading front leg positively thrust out, as if he's saying, 'I will go faster than these others,' and it is such an important attitude to have. A horse might have the breeding, the looks and the ability, but without that intangible quality, 'heart', and the will to win, he will never be a star, let alone a superstar.

And so the Derby beckoned but again not without a good deal of prior debate. John's cautious assessment was: 'He is by Cape Cross so there is a slight concern as to whether he will stay the mile and a half . . . but he is a half-brother to Galileo so there is plenty of stamina on the dam's side.' However, the paucity of Guineas winners going on to achieve the double meant that there were many who doubted he could pull it off.

It was a race I will never forget. For one thing, many young colts get extremely wound up on Derby Day. The sense of occasion is tangible. There are crowds everywhere, not just the well-dressed men and women in the enclosures, but the Epsom Downs on the far side are full of noise and laughter, with coach-loads of happy and possibly well-inebriated punters, gesticulating bookmakers calling the odds, a revolving 'big wheel' as part of a funfair: it is all there. There is also tension in the air among the human contestants and this can be easily transmitted to their young charges. Often it is warm on that first Saturday in June,

leading to colts getting fractious and 'boiling over' – and leaving any hope of winning in tatters. Amid this maelstrom, Sea The Stars and his trainer remained cool and calm.

The weather in June 2009 was not going to be hot and sunny; rain was forecast. Should John let his star run? About the only certainty was that the finish would involve Irish horses, for seven of the twelve runners were from Ireland and five of them headed the bookmakers' list – but not Sea The Stars. Not yet for him superstar status. There was not long to wait.

It was O'Brien's Fame And Glory who was the favourite, a horse that was to come into Sea The Stars' life again. Sea The Stars was 11–4 and then came his old rivals, Rip Van Winkle at 6–1, Black Bear Island at 7–1, and Gan Amhras at 8–1. O'Brien had six runners altogether. However, instead of letting them come into the parade ring one by one, after they were saddled, he waited until all six were ready and had their lads bring them into the paddock together, so late that spectators barely had a chance to see them. It denied the public not only an opportunity to admire, scrutinise and compare, but time enough afterwards to get to the bookmakers or to find a place on the stand. Aidan O'Brien was duly fined later.

Having enjoyed the privilege of seeing Sea The Stars at home meant that my eyes, glued to the television, were on him from the start. It didn't look too good at first. Sea The Stars was pulling wildly, throwing his head up in the air, trying to evade Mick Kinane's efforts to restrain him. Being the horseman he is, Mick soon had him relaxed and running well within himself, but the fear had to be that, given the doubts over his stamina, he would have used up too much energy in fighting.

A big horse can also find it harder to cope with Epsom's gradients and, in particular, the infamous bend called Tattenham Corner, around

The Epsom Derby, June 2009. Sea The Stars passes the post ahead of Fame And Glory and Masterofthehorse, two of Aidan O'Brien's six runners.

which many an immature three-year-old's hopes of immortality have been dashed. Sea The Stars had no such problems for he was perfectly balanced as he galloped round the corner and headed down the hill. From there on, on the heels of the leaders, he never looked in danger and took the lead a full furlong out, looking strong at the finish. All doubts about stamina vanished.

Golden Sword, one of Aidan O'Brien's two pacemakers, ran a wonderful race, being denied a place in only the last few yards by Fame And Glory, Masterofthehorse and Rip Van Winkle – three top-class horses who had been made to look ordinary.

Not only was the manner of Sea The Stars' victory perfect in every way but his jockey, too, had shown exactly why he had been in the top echelons for three decades – and the preparation by his meticulous trainer was faultless. John Oxx told the press, 'For once there were no anxious moments. Mick was delaying [his run] for as long as possible because the horse idles a bit in front. He's a terrific horse to have about the place. He's so straightforward, always in the same form. He's a big masculine presence. He owns the place and it's a pleasure looking at

*Being led to the winners'
enclosure after the Epsom
Derby, June 2009.*

him . . . He's a trouble-free horse, and we've rarely had an anxious moment. With any Guineas winner you'd be worried about staying a mile and a half, especially as he coasted the whole way in the Guineas and didn't just scramble there at the finish.'

After the Derby, Sea The Stars was estimated to be worth £40 million. By the end of the season, even that huge price tag was to look small.

Mick Kinane was fulsome in his praise for the new superstar, saying, 'Every step of the way I was winning today. I was a little worried he was over-racing a bit because he just found the pace too slow. . . . It was never in any doubt. I didn't think anything was going to beat me coming from behind. This horse has given me a new lease of life. I thought they'd go a shade quicker, but I don't think they could. . . . He broke so well that I thought I might have to sit right in behind the pacemakers. He was just coasting, he has so much class. I knew the pacemakers had both won their trials well, so they'd take me to the furlong marker.'

The *Racing Post* analysis noted: 'The winning margin was not extravagant, but it was a performance of sheer class and one that places Sea The Stars among the sport's true greats.'

Chapter 9

July, August and September 2009 – Undefeated

9

Sea The Stars had now won

two of racing's ancient Classics, the 2000 Guineas and the Derby, on his first two runs of 2009. Inevitably the talk was, where next? John Oxx told the press, 'We'd have to have a go at the Irish Derby if the ground were suitable, and after that, there are several very good mile-and-a-quarter races, but it all has yet to be discussed. If the ground at the Curragh is not suitable, then he could go for the Eclipse.' Punters therefore needed to be wary about backing Sea The Stars ante-post for the King George or the Arc, for which he was quoted at short prices, as neither was included in Plan A.

The Derby had taken place on 6 June and the Irish Derby was pencilled in for 28 June, making the two races fairly close together but not unreasonably so. Nothing was set in stone; should the ground come up soft at the Curragh, Sea The Stars would not be running in front of his by now devoted home crowd. As the rain fell it was touch-and-go.

But, it was not to be. John Oxx left the decision until the last possible moment and in the end he felt the ground was too soft. It was a bitterly disappointing blow for all concerned, including the Curragh racecourse and the Derby sponsors, Dubai Duty Free, who had also been denied the favourite running the previous year when New Approach pulled out late.

ABOVE, BELOW AND OPPOSITE ABOVE: *As they approach the final furlong, Aidan O'Brien's Rip Van Winkle appears ready to pass but Sea The Stars ups a gear and moves clear by a length.*

Most of all, the Irish public felt it. The hats had been got out and dusted, the pretty outfits readied and the legions who simply wanted to see a great horse in the flesh, Irish-bred, trained and ridden, were all disappointed. John Oxx was acutely aware of this; nevertheless, the horse's needs came first. Instead, Fame And Glory gained compensation for his earlier defeats by the Star.

Sea The Stars was destined for Sandown instead, and for the first time he would be racing against older horses. It was here that he was to give his fans their biggest concern yet; gone for ever were the days of Sea The Stars being odds against. For the remainder of his career he always started an odds-on favourite. Nine horses lined up against him on perfect ground at Sandown for the ten-furlong Coral Eclipse Stakes on 4 July. Two of Aidan O'Brien's runners were in as pacemakers for Rip Van Winkle, while Sir Michael Stoute also had a pacemaker in for Conduit. The big guns were readied. It is at times like these that an odds-on favourite, running over a new distance and against older horses for the first time, can be overturned, especially as in this instance the line-up also included Cima de Triomphe, winner of the Italian Derby and Conduit, winner of the St Leger, and the Breeders' Cup Turf.

Once the pacemakers had performed their task, Sea The Stars moved smoothly into the lead with two furlongs still to run. Rip Van Winkle, ridden by Jimmy Fortune, didn't let Star out of his sight and settled down to make a race of it. He forged closer and closer and reached his quarters, his girths, his neck; Mick Kinane went for his whip and spectators gasped. The upstart rival looked about to go past the star. Was the unthinkable about to happen? Not a bit of it; sensing the challenge, Sea The Stars simply went into overdrive and accelerated clear, finishing an easy length in front of Rip Van Winkle and with the rest spread out down the Sandown straight.

Afterwards Mick Kinane said, 'When the second horse came at me, he just picked up. You're never going to win by more than two lengths on him. He just does enough – he can only get better.' He felt the horse had been 'dossing' in front and doing no more than he had to. Mick admitted he had gone to the front earlier than he had wanted to but added, 'I just couldn't take a pull, he was travelling so well. It just turned out that there weren't enough good horses in front of him, so he ended up in front too early.'

BELOW: *Acknowledging the crowd – again, The Coral Eclipse, July 2009.*

Asked for his pre-race instructions, Oxx said he had told Kinane to

kick on and win by as far as possible, but Mick had replied, 'You must be joking! He'll never win by more than a length and a half.'

John Oxx said, 'I don't think he has a best distance. He can do them all.'

After the race, bookmakers William Hill offered odds on the colt going through the season undefeated at 5–1 . . .

John Oxx named the Irish Champion Stakes, at Leopardstown on 5 September, as Sea The Stars' main target for the rest of the year, with

In the ring before the race, the Juddmonte International Stakes, York, August 2009.

the usual caveat: ground permitting. Sea The Stars was likely to have one run before then, in either Ascot's King George at the end of July or the Juddmonte International at York three weeks later in August. Oxx added, 'We are not really seriously considering the Arc for him, although he is in it.'

York turned out to be the next race. Traditionally the 'Royal Ascot' of the North, it is well worthy of the accolade; indeed, in June 2005, York stood in for Royal Ascot while the Berkshire course was undergoing refurbishment. Again the race was over ten furlongs, and was once more against older horses. But by now gamesmanship was coming into play and opposition camps – the Ballydoyle camp in particular – were trying all they could within the bounds of racing rules to see if or how they could trip up the favourite.

Sea The Stars had run in May, June and July, and had won each time. Many top horses would now be given a break, a short summer holiday, especially if they had important autumn engagements. But Sea The Stars needed to run; an idle life was not for him. Only five runners of eight original entries stood their ground. When one of those pulled out overnight, this left four – and the other three were trained by Aidan O'Brien. The crowds flocked to York's attractive and historic racecourse, close to the River Ouse, eager to see the Star in action.

The spectators admired his muscular presence and gleaming coat in the paddock and his athletic stride as he cantered easily down to the ten-furlong starting post. The ground was good-to-firm and his price was 4–1 on. Lined up alongside him were Mastercraftsman at 3–1, along with Georgebernardshaw at 100–1 and Set Sail at 125–1.

This time Sea The Stars stayed tucked in behind the leaders longer than he had before, to the consternation of many in the packed stands. Georgebernardshaw did his job for the first mile and then Set Sail took over. Mastercraftsman swept into the lead fully two furlongs from home. His two pacemakers were now behind him and Sea The Stars was behind them. Was he going to be boxed in? Tension was acute in the stands.

But they hadn't reckoned on the experience of Mick Kinane or – many not having seen him before – the superlative ability of Sea The Stars. Mick pulled him up to the pack and doglegged through a gap to be right on the heels of Mastercraftsman, and then gave him a pull, a remarkable thing to be able to do in a Group One race, but Mick didn't want to take on the

OVERLEAF: The 2009 Juddmonte International Stakes. The moment when Sea The Stars passes Masterofthehorse to go on to win by a length.

leader too soon. To the layman, unaware of what the skilful jockey was doing, it looked for a few moments as if he couldn't go with the leader. Not a bit of it. When Mick deemed the moment right, with a shake of the reins and a flick of the whip, the pair swept by – and once again Sea The Stars won his race by a length, the other two horses some distance behind. The crowds erupted and ran towards the winner's enclosure to welcome in the superstar. The time of the race was announced – a new course record.

For Irish racing fans in particular, 5 September 2009 will long be remembered. 'Their' Star was to run in the Tattersalls Millions Irish Champion Stakes at Leopardstown – or so they hoped. All the preceding week, as the unprecedented rainfall of July and August began to subside, John Oxx kept in close touch with Leopardstown racecourse; the forecast was not particularly good. On the Friday, the day before the race, John walked the course – and was pleasantly surprised with what he found. The horse was declared to run.

BELOW: *The crowd looks down into the ring at Leopardstown before the Tattersalls Millions Irish Championship Stakes, September 2009.*

Tension before the start at Leopardstown, September 2009.

Crowds flocked in their thousands to the southern suburb of Dublin. One of the most memorable Irish Champion Stakes of recent years was in 2001 when Fantastic Light lowered the colours of the hitherto unbeaten Galileo, by a head.

Might it happen again? Unthinkable! Yet the ground was officially declared good-to-yielding for the ten-furlong race. As ever, Aidan O'Brien had lined up a range of horses to take on Sea The Stars, including Fame And Glory (9–4). Mastercraftsman (6–1) was in again, along with O'Brien's outsiders Grand Ducal at 100–1, Set Sail, ridden by Aidan's son Joseph, and Rockhampton, both on 150–1. Sea The Stars not only had to beat a couple of good horses; he also had to avoid trouble as five of the runners were rank outsiders.

It was a marvellous race to watch. Set Sail duly lived up to his name, and by the time the business end of the race was reached, Mastercraftsman assumed the lead, if briefly, before Fame And Glory took over. Was the

ABOVE: *Once again Aidan O'Brien's Fame And Glory is the challenger but is convincingly beaten by two and a half lengths in the 2009 Tattersalls Millions Irish Championship Stakes.*

BELOW: *Tucked in behind the frontrunners, Sea The Stars and Mick Kinane bide their time.*

*Celebrations and trophies.
The third win out of three
in 2009 . . .*

Irish Derby winner going to cause an upset to the Star? Suddenly there
was the champion, racing smoothly past his rivals and taking the lead
fully a furlong out. He galloped to a victory that he made look easy, and
this time his winning margin was two lengths.

After the race, an unusually bullish John Oxx called his horse the
best by far, adding, 'He'll win the Arc.'

And so the scene was set. The Prix de l'Arc de Triomphe at Longchamp
was to be Sea The Stars' biggest challenge.

Chapter 10

October 2009 –
Winning the Arc

10

The Arc,

as the Lucien Barrière Prix de l'Arc de Triomphe is affectionately known, is not only Europe's richest horse race (in 2009 worth a staggering 10.5 million French francs – about £1.5 million – shared between the top five horses, of which approximately £850,000 goes to the winner) but it is also a 'must' in many English and Irish racegoers' calendars. This was never more so than in October 2009.

The Longchamp racecourse, built in the Bois de Boulogne in the heart of Paris on the banks of the River Seine, covers more than forty acres of interlocking racetracks. Ever since the Emperor Napoleon III, his wife Eugénie and a host of fashionable racing aficionados attended the first day of racing there in 1857, it has been a wonderful mix of the beau monde – many displaying truly eclectic taste – the bourgeoisie and dedicated followers of racing from all over the world. Like the Epsom and Kentucky Derbys or Royal Ascot, it has remained a feast of fashion combined with the highest-class racing. Traditionally held on the first Sunday in October, it quickly established itself as the end-of-season European championship for horses aged three years and older over the classic distance of a mile and a half. As the last major race of

ABOVE: *Noura Mohammed Al-Khulaifi of the Virginia Commonwealth University in Qatar showing off her winning design for the Prix de l'Arc de Triomphe. It was made in Milan in gold and pearls with a malachite base.*

BELOW: *Some of the large Irish contingent which flew to Paris before the Arc.*

the flat season, it regularly attracts the best horses in the world. Since many will go on to stud the following year, the outcome of the race has an important part to play in determining the price a stallion will subsequently command.

As he observed Sea The Stars' progress through the season, John Oxx had gone from stating earlier in the summer that the horse was most unlikely to run in the Arc to asserting that he would win it. Sea The Stars had just kept getting better and after the Champion Stakes he had an official rating higher than any other horse in the world.

Thousands of English and Irish racegoers swelled the crowds at Longchamp that sunny afternoon of Sunday, 4 October 2009, along with people from many other parts of the world, including the Middle East and especially Qatar. The Arc has always attracted world-class sponsors and this was to be the second of a five-year contract with the state of Qatar. Earlier in the year, design students from the School of Arts of the Virginia Commonwealth University, in Qatar, entered a competition to design the 2009 trophies for the Qatar-sponsored Arc. Apparently there is no word for 'design' in Arabic. Nevertheless, in June 2009 twenty-one female students became the first in the state – as well as in the Gulf region – to receive their Bachelor of Fine Arts degree. The winner of the competition was nineteen-year-old Noura Mohammed

Al-Khulaifi. The only regret, both for her and for her American tutor, Kathleen Ferguson Huntington, was that they were unable to make it to Paris for the race.

x

And what a race. This was the day Sea The Stars truly proved himself a giant of world racing, not just of this era but of any. How I longed to be in Longchamp as I stewarded a fence for a local point-to-point in Ireland. Fortunately, an away bookmaker had taken his television along with him and I ensured I was at the front of the ever-swelling crowd to watch the race.

It was one that brought flooding back memories of Dawn Run's French Champion Hurdle win at Auteuil. Before that race there had been persistent rumours (unjustified, I hasten to add) that the French were out to 'do' the famous mare. She shrugged that off by simply galloping to the front and staying there throughout the race. No other horse, French or otherwise, ever got anywhere close to her as she galloped and jumped her heart out in the Auteuil sunshine.

Now, twenty-five years later in another part of Paris, eighteen opponents lined up against the superstar, Europe's elite along with the usual number of pacemakers. It is a sign of the esteem in which the Star was now held that after his odds of 4–6, the next nearest was his old rival Fame And Glory on 6–1. Michael Stoute's Conduit was at 8–1.

Moving to the start, the Prix de l'Arc de Triomphe, Longchamp, October 2009.

A French-trained trio comprised Cavalryman at 12–1 ridden by Frankie Dettori, Vision D'Etat at 14–1, and Beheshtam at 16–1. On at 20–1 was Youmzain for Mick Channon, a six-year-old who had finished runner-up in both the previous two Arcs.

After them the two talented fillies, John Gosden's Dar Re Mi and the French Stacelita, were both on 20–1 and the German Getaway was on 33–1. Other than that, the prices of the remainder ranged through 150–1, 250–1, 300–1 and even 500–1. One of five on the latter odds, La Boum, did well to dead-heat for seventh but the rest proved to be realistically priced.

However, the vast majority of eyes that day were for Sea The Stars only. For the first and only time in his career, he sweated a little in the preliminaries and when at last they were under way he could be seen desperately fighting Mick Kinane for his head. It was like the Derby again but worse. Eventually Mick got him settled but in doing so he was now way back in ninth place against the rail with a host of horses ahead and to the side of him. With a mass of horses surrounding him, could he, when the moment came, not only extricate himself but also have

The field in the 2009 Arc. As they enter the last third of the race, Sea The Stars begins to reel in the pacemakers.

enough speed and stamina to go on and win a race as prestigious as the Arc, or would the other jockeys close him in? My heart was in my mouth along with countless thousands of others.

The pacemakers had gone so far clear that in truth the real race was being led by Stacelita, ridden by Christophe Soumillon, and Dar Re Mi with Jimmy Fortune. Sea The Stars was on the inside and looked completely boxed in. But slowly, inexorably, he pulled through the throng to join the leaders. Although it still looked an impossible task, he changed gear again to sweep imperiously past the front runners, leaving them toiling in his wake as he ran clear to win by two lengths.

In a trice the point-to-point crowd turned from nail-biting silence to a sea of people jumping up and down and embracing each other, tears flowing freely. It was one of the greatest moments in horse-racing life.

Television shows the race clearly, but for the atmosphere of being there on the day I am indebted to Mark Costello, deputy editor of the *Irish Field*, who gave me his own colourful recollection:

'I had been to the Arc twice before, and seen two great winners in Sinndar in 2000 and Dalakhani in 2003. By coincidence both were

Moving beautifully, as always, Sea The Stars has hit the front in the 2009 Arc.

owned by the Aga Khan and of course Sinndar was trained by John Oxx.

'Watching the 2008 Arc from home on television, I was stunned to see the Aga Khan's unbeaten filly Zarkava get out of an impossible position on the rails and fly home to win by two lengths. I thought to myself that I should have been there, to see what may have been the best Arc winner of all time. Little did I or anyone else think that there would be an even better winner the very next year!

'One of my strongest memories from Arc day in 2009 was how warm and sunny it was. Irish visitors were in real danger of getting sunburned. The parade ring area is full of champagne bars and there were Irish voices everywhere. I noticed that quite a few Irish racegoers did not know much about racing, but they regularly attended this meeting, maybe as a holiday.

'I didn't go down to the parade ring beforehand but I understand that a round of applause broke out just as Sea The Stars entered the area. It has been reported that the horse was noticeably warm in the preliminaries and he certainly gave a few bucks on the way to the start, as this was shown in slow motion on the big screens in front of the grandstand.

'There is a very good viewing area in the grandstand for journalists so I went up there and sat beside Brough Scott and Sean Magee – giants of the racing writing world. I remember reading Brough's account of Dancing Brave's Arc win in the *Racing Post* in 1986 and tingling with excitement as he described the winner's devastating burst of speed, which took him past a host of top-class racehorses.

'Back to Sunday: as the last horses were being loaded into the stalls, everyone rose from their seats and a big roar went up as the field broke away. With two French commentators sharing microphone duties, I found it almost impossible to follow the action, though I knew the colours of just about all the jockeys. The camerawork in France is also a bit erratic – you could call it artistic – and so even watching the big screen didn't tell you all you wanted to know.

'Still, it was obvious that Aidan O'Brien's outsiders were haring off in front and had opened a gap of about ten lengths on the others by halfway. Sea The Stars was about halfway back in the field of nineteen runners, racing on the inside. I didn't know it at the time but he had been racing a bit keenly and had been involved in a bit of bumping too.

'Turning into the long home straight, the French filly Stacelita swallowed up the tiring pacemakers and appeared to shoot clear. The home fans were screaming and, for a moment, I couldn't see the yellow and purple silks of Michael Kinane anywhere – he was a bit boxed in on the rails and my heart sank. It looked as if he would probably finish only fifth or sixth. There would be the usual excuses – a race too many, he didn't settle, he had no luck, he just didn't fire.

'But then, in a flash, Michael Kinane switched Sea The Stars off the rails and the horse took off. It was a bit like Zarkava a year earlier.

'I was shouting now ("Yes, go on! Go on!") and, very quickly, it became obvious that the momentum of Sea The Stars would take him past the now tiring Stacelita well before the finishing line. Furthermore, the eye could see that none of the other runners was finishing quite as fast either, so victory was assured.

'I began clapping and cheering but also trying to savour the moment in slow motion and record the images on to the brain's hard drive, never to be deleted.

'There was a hell of a buzz through the grandstand. Many racegoers started to dash for the parade ring and the winner's enclosure, but I stayed in the stand as I knew Sea The Stars would be paraded all the way back in front of us. It was fun to watch his groom John Hynes, head man Slim O'Neill and travelling head lad Jeff Houlihan embrace each other on the track below me and walk down to meet the returning

OVERLEAF ABOVE: *A sequence showing Sea The Stars (reading right to left) clear of the field as he passes the finishing post.*

OVERLEAF BELOW: *Having moved from near the back, threaded his way through the traffic and hunted down the leaders – who were at one stage at least ten lengths ahead of the pack – Sea The Stars surges clear to win the Arc, October 2009.*

horse and jockey. I wondered what they might be saying to each other. What a year they have had. What memories.

'After they had collected the heroes of the hour, the entourage duly paraded past the stands, the sponsor's rug already on the horse's quarters. As they went behind the stand to the parade ring, somebody gave the jockey an Irish flag and he held it aloft as he was led into the

ABOVE: *After the Arc a clearly emotional Mick Kinane draped in the Irish tricolour is led in to the winners' enclosure.*

RIGHT: *Sea The Stars, 'not at all fazed', is patted by groom Johnny Hynes and Mick Kanine.*

winner's enclosure. I was watching from the back of the stand, through a glass wall, so I couldn't hear how loud the cheers were.

'The horse went out of my sight for a while but I imagine that he was not at all fazed by the atmosphere or the crowds in the ring. I noticed that at Leopardstown after his previous race: he just stands there like a statue, totally bomb-proof, and I don't think it is because he is exhausted.

'An odd thing happened then – something that I think is unique to the Arc. Three horse-drawn carriages arrived in the parade ring to take the jockey, trainer, owner and other connections back out on to the track for the official presentation. The horse was presumably taken in a different direction, to the stables, to be drug-tested.

'In front of the stands, right by the winning post, the presentation ceremony takes place. At Longchamp the highlight of the ceremony is the performance of the national anthem of the winning country. Again, that is very unusual after a horse race – more like Croke Park on All-Ireland day. It all added to the sense of occasion and made every Irish person there, and those watching from home, feel a bit special.'

ABOVE: *He wasn't to know it but this was to be a final farewell from Mick Kinane.*

BELOW: *Mick Kinane, Christopher Tsui and John Oxx stand as the Irish National anthem is played, Longchamp, October 2009.*

Chapter 11

After the Arc

It takes a while to come down

from a high such as the 2009 Arc, the culmination of a momentous season that catapulted Sea The Stars into the limelight. After the Arc, to emphasise his extraordinary qualities, his trainer said: 'The horse has never been better. He's never been fitter, he's never been stronger. He was full of running at the end when they wanted to pull him up. It was his easiest win!' He had simply flown past his strong-running competitors towards the end of the race.

Immediately after the Arc in the very next race at Longchamp, John Oxx saddled the Aga Khan's Alandi and Mick Kinane rode him to yet another victory, this time beating Kasbah Bliss by a head. Only then could the celebrations begin in earnest.

For Christopher Tsui, the Arc was an extraordinary moment. He had been a young schoolboy sixteen years earlier in 1993 when he had watched Urban Sea, his parents' mare and Sea The Stars' dam, win the same race. 'I really never dreamed that I would one day myself stand here at Longchamp and see my colours aboard an Arc de Triomphe winner. It's a very emotional moment.'

As always, he watched the race linked up to an iPhone, relaying the progress of the race to his mother because, he told the press, out of superstition neither she nor his father ever come racing.

Mick Kinane, Christopher Tsui and Sea The Stars after the 2009 Derby.

'An extraordinary horse!' he said after it was over. 'My mother was very nervous and she is now overjoyed. She's afraid of coming to the races. She's afraid of seeing him run. These are nerve-racking moments for her, but she follows everything from home on television and she is thrilled.'

Christopher Tsui takes superstition seriously and the luck it might bring, always wearing the same suit and red tie, and hosting a pre-race lunch for eight people on table eight – wherever they might be. Eight is a lucky number in China and after the race he noted, 'This is the eighty-eighth edition of the Arc. He [Sea the Stars] had number 18 and was stabled in stall number 84; we watched the race from box 128; and even on the plane, flying in, I was seated in seat 18.'

The staff of Curraghbeg show Sea The Stars to the press after the Arc.

For Mick Kinane, used to riding top-flight horses all over the world, Sea The Stars was 'simply the best. An extraordinary talent who is a

pleasure to ride. A horse that comes along only once in a lifetime.'

John Oxx called Sea The Stars a fairytale horse, the Usain Bolt of the horse-racing world, a fantastic athlete with acceleration to dream of, who kept on improving and was mentally strong. He had been asked to perform in excess of the normal – six major races in six months – but he was an exceptional horse who was capable of taking it, indeed seemed to thrive on it. After the Arc, Oxx said, 'We are lucky and privileged to have a horse like this. He's a great, great horse to keep on winning and to have won all of those races.'

Ordinary racegoers had their say, too:

'He's a proper champion. He was never in trouble – you don't get in trouble when you have those sorts of gears.'

'He is superb, different class to anything else. He was the best bet of the day.'

Caitriona and John Oxx with John Hynes, Sea The Stars and staff at Curraghbeg.

Sea The Stars at Curraghbeg with his blankets from each of the Classics. A photocall for the international press.

'What a tremendous horse! He met trouble in running and pulled hard, but he overcame it all like only a tremendous horse can. We will be lucky to see another one as good.'

One of the more unusual post-Arc outcomes was that, following requests from punters, Paddy Power added Sea The Stars to the RTE 1 Irish 'Sports Personality of the Year' betting. On both sides of the Irish Sea he was automatic favourite for racing awards, such as the prestigious Cartier Awards, not to mention the torrent of accolades that poured in from breeders' organisations and the press.

The debate about whether or not to run in the Breeders' Cup on 7 November was intense. It is at times like these that such a horse becomes public property and every man and woman in the street has their own opinion. John Oxx himself insisted that no decision would be made for at least a week and a half, to see how the Star would settle post his Paris exertions. In fact he came home in his usual fine fettle and the familiar equine figure to lads from other yards was soon to be seen cantering out on the Curragh in the early mornings.

He was odds-on favourite 'with a run' for America; if he were to win a seventh Group One in a row, in seven consecutive months, it would be truly unprecedented. The pot was $5 million and therefore tempting in anyone's book. But John Oxx's self-control concerning the welfare of his horses is always paramount, even in the face of enormous pressure. He had not run the horse in the Irish Derby, much as he personally would have loved to win it again, and moreover he was well aware of the disappointment the decision caused to Irish racing. The temptation to go on was there; the horse had never been stronger or fitter.

John Oxx wasn't ruling it out but was not going to be pressured into a decision. The horse had originally been entered in the Breeders' Cup only as a fall-back, should the going turn soft at Longchamp.

Again, Joe Public joined the debate along with the experts. Websites and chat rooms were alive with opinions for and against. On the 'for' side:

'If I owned a horse like Sea The Stars I would run him in the Classic. I would also keep him in training as a four-year-old. If all was well, I'd aim him at the Dubai World Cup and perhaps another tilt at the Arc again. He has nothing to lose but a few races.'

'Should he win the Classic, he would be the only Arc winner ever to have won a Breeders' Cup race. Think of it! Seven Classic races won in seven months! Yes, there's a reputation at risk. But really, he's the best, and the best always find a way to win. He's much better than Ravens Pass [the 2008 winner], he can win it easy!'

'Risk what exactly? He is not unbeaten, not over-raced and Mick Kinane said that the Arc was his easiest win. Some things you have to do for the sport and this is one. Send him over.'

Those 'against' said:

'After what happened to George Washington [killed in the Breeders' Cup] I fail to see the point in sending Sea The Stars . . . He doesn't have anything to prove and you don't need the best horse in the world to have to run in the Breeders' Cup Classic to prove the point.'

'It was stated yesterday that Sea The Stars had started to "go" in his coat. That should tell his connections that "enough is enough". Sea The Stars has nothing to gain, but he has a fantastic/brilliant reputation to lose by going to the States.'

OVERLEAF: *Sea The Stars at home at Curraghbeg after the Arc, October 2009.*

Those in the business chimed in too. One of them, the American trainer Chip Woolley Junior, had trained Mine That Bird to a 50–1 win in the 2009 Kentucky Derby where he had won by nearly seven lengths from being sixteen lengths down at one stage, and had entered his horse for the Breeders' Cup. Woolley said Sea The Stars would be a 'monster' if he came over. The Santa Anita venue, naturally, was also eager for him to come for the 10,000 or so extra people it would attract.

Refreshingly, Christopher Tsui made it clear that, in spite of receiving many very big offers, it was his intention to keep the horse in family ownership, and at stud in Ireland.

Nine days after the Arc, Sea The Stars' retirement was announced and his chosen stud shortly afterwards. It was to be the Aga Khan's Gilltown stud in Co. Kildare and in a neat symmetry among the first mares Sea The Stars will cover is the Aga Khan's Zarkava, the previous winner of the Arc. Slated to cover about 120 mares in his first season at €85,000 a time he will generate over €50 million in net income over three years.

For Sea The Stars, life was to go on as usual for a little while; he would still canter on the Curragh, but he would not be having work gallops to build up to yet another race. John Oxx and Sea The Stars' lad, John Hynes, could gaze at their charge across the springy expanse of Curragh turf in pure admiration.

As John Oxx told me, 'It is wonderful to have been on the journey with him.'

OPPOSITE: *Irish through and through: foaled at the Irish National Stud, trained in Ireland and now to stand at stud in Ireland. Sea The Stars has even been entered for RTE's 'Sports Personality of the Year'. He may well win . . .*

BELOW: *Sea The Stars with his stablemates at Curraghbeg.*

Chapter 12
The Best Ever?

12

Comparisons, however impossible

to prove between generations, come as an inevitable sideshow to a superstar.

The horse that has perhaps most often been compared to Sea The Stars is Nijinsky, the last horse ever to win the Triple Crown of the 2000 Guineas, the Derby and the St Leger, in 1970. However, times have changed since then; commercial flat breeders want ever more speed and so winners of the St Leger, because of its longer distance, are inclined to get sent off to stud as National Hunt stallions, at considerably cheaper fees, making them a less valuable piece of equine property.

Hailed by many as the 'horse of the century' (the twentieth), Nijinsky was by Northern Dancer and, like him, was to spawn a dynasty as a stallion. Not least of his progeny was Sadler's Wells, who took over the mantle of leading sire and, on his retirement, passed on his prowess to his son, Galileo, half-brother to Sea The Stars. First, however, Nijinsky had to prove himself outstanding on the track, and to begin with he looked like being his own worst enemy. He had a volatile temperament and was difficult to handle as a youngster but once he reached the racecourse he became the champion two-year-old of both England and Ireland. Occasionally, when a precocious two-year-old does not do enough maturing, a horse may fail to 'train on' at three, but Nijinsky maintained his form in no uncertain fashion: with Lester Piggott he

OPPOSITE: *Winning in fine style: the 2009 2000 Guineas.*

won the 2000 Guineas, a high-class Derby, the Irish Derby and the King George in stunning fashion. In short, he appeared invincible.

Although between the King George and the St Leger he contracted ringworm, whose treatment alone can take a lot out of a horse, Nijinsky nevertheless won the Leger, becoming the first horse since Bahram in 1935 to win the elusive Triple Crown. He therefore became the favourite in 1970 to take the Arc, just as was Sea The Stars in 2009.

Sea The Stars did not contest the St Leger, officially because of doubts about his stamina. John Oxx was quoted as saying, 'We thought long and hard about whether he'd get the Derby trip and if I'd said to Mick we were thinking about running in the St Leger he'd be worried we were losing our marbles.'

My own belief is that Sea The Stars could have won the Leger doing handstands, no matter that he's by a miler. He would barely have been out of third gear against inferior opposition.

The Champion Stakes at Newmarket could perhaps be called the modern-day last leg of the British Triple Crown but for one important difference: it is open to all ages and is therefore not a Classic for three-year-olds. The Prix de l'Arc de Triomphe, Europe's leading race, comes in at roughly the same time as the third leg of the Triple Crown – and Sea The Stars became the first horse ever to win that alongside the 2000 Guineas and the Derby.

For Nijinsky, the Arc was not to be; even though he had swept all before him that season, he lost the Arc by a head. There are many who still blame his jockey, the inimitable Lester Piggott, for his defeat, but then he was beaten again at the Champion Stakes.

Back in the 1950s the Italian colt Ribot was unbeaten in sixteen races over three seasons, including two Arcs. Yet none of those wins included a Classic. And he could be temperamental, a trait he was inclined to pass down to his progeny. Nevertheless, as a racehorse in his era he reigned supreme.

The 1960s and 1970s produced a plethora of colts with genuine credentials to vie for the tag of 'the greatest'. In 1965 the French-trained Sea-Bird II won the Derby and beat a high-class Arc field with consummate ease. Until Sea The Stars came along, the distinctive chestnut was for many the best they had ever seen.

A few years later, Sir Ivor appeared unbeatable, only to lose races before the end of his career. Sir Ivor's 'Classic' year was 1968, two years before Nijinsky's, and like that horse he was trained by Vincent O'Brien. His owner, Raymond Guest, was American ambassador to Ireland, whose L'Escargot won successive Cheltenham Gold Cups in 1970–71, followed in 1975 by victory in the Grand National at Aintree.

Like Sea The Stars, Sir Ivor finished fourth on his debut and then remained unbeaten as a two-year-old. Like the Star, after Sir Ivor won the 2000 Guineas as a three-year-old there was much debate about whether his pedigree had given him enough stamina for him to also win the Derby – but he did. He was, however, defeated in the Irish Derby, the Eclipse and the Arc, redeeming himself by winning not only the Champion Stakes but also the Washington DC International in America, a return to form that showed real strength of character.

Brigadier Gerard was almost to emulate Ribot, winning his first fifteen races and losing only his last. He was born in the same year as Derby winner Mill Reef, although the only time they met was in the 2000 Guineas in 1971 when the Brigadier won against Mill Reef and My Swallow by an imperious three lengths. However, connections did not believe he had the stamina, on breeding, for the Derby – think how close John Oxx came to a similar conclusion for Sea The Stars – and so he did not run. Therefore, Brigadier Gerard had the first Classic, and as a four-year-old he added to his impressive curriculum vitae the Eclipse and the Arc. He suffered his sole defeat at the Benson & Hedges Gold Cup at York, being beaten by the 1972 Derby winner Roberto who broke the course record to do so.

Mill Reef, having been beaten by the Brigadier in the 2000 Guineas, won the Derby, the Eclipse, the King George and the Arc as a three-year-old. He also stayed in training as a four-year-old, winning impressively in France, but he and Brigadier Gerard never met again after the initial 2000 Guineas.

The ill-fated Shergar was a distinctive horse with his four white socks and broad white blaze. His two runs at the age of two both produced a first and, in a Group One race, a second. When he reached the age of three there was no stopping him. It wasn't just that he kept winning, but that he kept doing so by record margins in record times. One of Sea The Stars' traits is that he wins only by so much, 'idling' when in front; in contrast, Shergar was one of those rare racing machines revelled in solo glory. Memorably, he won the 1981 Derby by a record ten lengths in near bottomless ground, and followed up with four-length victories in both the Irish Derby and the King George. After a summer break, he came back for the St. Leger and was a well-beaten fourth. Sadly, the following year when standing at stud in Ireland, he was kidnapped by masked gunmen who attempted to ransom him. He was never seen again.

Another horse of sheer quality in that decade – although comparable with those of any era – was Dancing Brave, winner in 1986 of the 2000 Guineas, the King George, the Eclipse and, after a summer break, the Arc. The only blot on his copybook was just failing in the Derby.

In recent times horses whose careers bear comparison with Sea The Stars include Galileo, Duke of Marmalade (winner of five Group Ones in 2007), Giant's Causeway (winner of five Group Ones in 2000), and Rock of Gibraltar – a miler – who, in the two seasons 2001–2, won seven consecutive Group Ones but was beaten in the Breeders' Cup. All of these horses wins included some narrow victories, unlike the authoritative ones of Sea The Stars.

Further back in history, the famous Eclipse was unbeaten in eighteen races (half of them walkovers) in the 1760s, becoming a phenomenally influential sire down the ages. Sceptre, a filly, won four of the five 1902 Classics. Pretty Polly, also influential in racing bloodlines, won the fillies' Triple Crown of 1904 and a total of twenty-two of her twenty-four races.

In a lower league, that of a handicapper, one of the greatest flat-racing mares of all time was Makybe Diva; conceived in Ireland by Desert King, she was born in England and raced in Australia. When she was bidding for her third consecutive Melbourne Gold Cup – the day the whole of Australia annually comes to a standstill – I set the alarm for 3 a.m., slept on the sofa and woke to witness via television one of the great racing moments when she achieved her remarkable feat. It was one of the most memorable races I had ever seen – until Sea The Stars began his sequence. Twelve hours after that Melbourne Cup, on the other side of the world, Best Mate, triple winner of the Cheltenham Gold Cup, collapsed and died at Exeter.

Whilst I shall always remember Shergar's Derby win of 1981, as well as Lammtarra's Arc win of 1995 – his burnished chestnut coat shining in the Parisian sun; a bubbling Frankie Dettori – nothing can diminish the power, the presence and, like his trainer, the quiet authority of Sea The Stars.

My own pipedream, now for ever a dream, would have been for Sea The Stars to race on as a four-year-old.

Imagine another Arc, a King George, another Irish Champion Stakes . . . Imagine this equine athlete becoming even more perfect than he is today, with his stunning turn of speed, his superiority in every respect, his remarkable temperament, his ability to win at any distance and to turn up fit, sound and, above all, willing, month after month without a break. This superstar is without a single blemish.

Watching Sea The Stars has been a pleasure and a privilege. His Derby and Arc wins were unforgettable, and his Irish Champion Stakes just that: champion – simply the best.

BELOW: *The 2009 Tattersalls Millions, Leopardstown, where Sea The Stars won by two and a half lengths from Fame And Glory – his biggest winning margin. His acceleration was so quick, Plan A was to stay with the pack and wait until the last moment to release the brakes. His winning margins were therefore usually small.*

Race Statistics

Name: Sea The Stars	**Owner:** Christopher Tsui
Sire: Cape Cross	**Trainer:** John Oxx
Dam: Urban Sea	**Jockey:** Mick Kinane
Age: Three	**Retired:** October 13, 2009
Foaled: April 6, 2006 in Ireland	**Results:** nine starts, eight wins: 1 Maiden, 1 Group 2, 6 Group 1.

2008

1. Jebel Ali Stables EBF (C&G), Curragh (Maiden)
13.07.08 7 furlongs Good 18 ran

1. Driving Snow /CD Hayes (K Prendergast) 7/1
2. Black Bear Island / JA Heffernan (AP O'Brien) 10/1
3. Freemantle / JP Murtagh (AP O'Brien) 6/1
4. Sea The Stars / MJ Kinane (JM Oxx) 6/1

Sea The Stars first outing saw him start slowly in a large field but challenge strongly at the end, coming in fourth with the three in front a head, half a length and a neck ahead in a tight finish. Nonetheless the surge of acceleration which was to be his trademark was absent that day so the race offered few clues to his future as arguably the greatest racehorse the world has ever seen.

2. Korean Racing Authority European Breeders' Fund (C&G), Leopardstown (Maiden)
17.08.08 7 furlongs Heavy 14 ran

1. Sea The Stars / MJ Kinane (JM Oxx) 2/1 fav
2. Dark Humour / PJ Smullen (DK Weld) 13/2
3. The Bull Hayes / FM Berry (Mrs J Harrington) 8/1

His first win, despite soft going. In a field of fourteen he won with ease, two and a half lengths clear of Dark Humour and five lengths clear of The Bull Hayes.

3. Juddmonte Beresford Stakes, Curragh (Group 2)
28.09.08 8 furlongs Yielding 6 ran

1. Sea The Stars / MJ Kinnane (JM Oxx) 7/4
2. Mourayan / FM Berry (JM Oxx) 10/1
3. Masterofthehorse / (AP O'Brien) 11/8 fav

Moving up to Group 2 he finished half a length ahead of his stablemate, the Aga Khan's Mourayan who had won in July at Leopardstown by three lengths with Mick Kinane up.

2009

4. The stanjames.com 2000 Guineas Stakes, Newmarket (Group 1)
02.05.09 8 furlongs Good to Firm 15 ran

1. Sea The Stars / MJ Kinane (JM Oxx) 8-1
2. Delegator / JP Spencer (BJ Meehan) 3-1 fav
3. Gan Amhras / KJ Manning (JS Bolger) 15-2

Sea The Stars was tucked behind the leading horses as the field spread across the track. As his now trademark spurt took him to the front he was challenged hard by Delegator but easily found that extra gear to run past him to win by a length and a half.

5. Investec Derby, Epsom (Group 1)
06.06.09 12 furlongs Good 12 ran

1. Sea The Stars / MJ Kinane (JM Oxx) 11/4
2. Fame And Glory / (AP O'Brien) 9/4 fav
3. Masterofthehorse / (AP O'Brien) 16/1

At the mile Sea The Stars was running easily in fourth with Golden Sword and Age of Aquarius six lengths clear of the pack. With the pace quickening the leaders were hunted down and as the leading group bunched nearing the post Sea The Stars moved smoothly into the lead to win by one and three quarter lengths from Fame And Glory.

6. The Coral-Eclipse, Sandown (Group 1)
04.07.09 10 furlongs Good 10 ran

1. Sea The Stars / MJ Kinane (JM Oxx) 4/7 fav
2. Rip Van Winkle / J Fortune (AP O'Brien) 11/2
3. Conduit / R Moore (M Stoute) 9/2

A steady race in fifth or sixth position as the two pacemakers got away several lengths clear. At the straight Sea the Stars pulled ahead to be challenged hard by Rip Van Winkle who appeared to have the pace to pass him in the final furlong. But with another burst of speed Sea the Stars forged ahead and was out of danger to win by a length with Conduit four and a half lengths behind.

7. Juddmonte International Stakes, York (Group 1)
18.08.09 10 furlongs Good to Firm 4 ran

1. Sea The Stars / MJ Kinane (JM Oxx) 1/4 fav
2. Mastercraftsman / J Murtagh (AP O'Brien) 3/1
3. Set Sail / JA Heffernan (AP O'Brien) 100/1

Georgebernardshaw set the pace and at the halfway was four and a half lengths clear with Sea The Stars last in the field of four. As they headed for home Sea The Stars sidestepped through a gap and bore down on Mastercraftsman who responded strongly and appeared to have the speed to see him off but yet again Sea The Stars found another gear to sweep imperiously past him to win by a length.

8. Tattersalls Millions Irish Championship Stakes, Leopardstown (Group 1)
05.09.09 10 furlongs Good to Yielding 9 ran

1. Sea The Stars / MJ Kinane (JM Oxx) 4/6 fav
2. Fame And Glory / J Murtagh (AP O'Brien) 9/4
3. Mastercraftsman / JA Heffernan (AP O'Brien) 6/1

With five Aidan O'Brien-trained horses amongst the nine runners including multiple Group 1–winners Fame and Glory and Mastercraftsman there was some competition to beat. Sea The Stars was in his trademark position in the middle of the field at the halfway mark as Set Sail went clear by five to six lengths. Boxed in as they approached the straight he moved to the outside and sprinted clear unchallenged to win by two and a half lengths from Fame And Glory and five lengths clear of Mastercraftsman.

9. Prix de l'Arc de Triomphe, Longchamp (Group 1)
04.10.09 12 furlongs Good 19 ran

1. Sea The Stars / MJ Kinane (JM Oxx) 4/6 fav
2. Youmzain / K Fallon (MR Channon) 20/1
3. Cavalryman / F Dettori (A Fabre) 12/1

Unsettled in the first part of the race and as Mick Kinnane fought to rein him in he appeared to be losing ground fast as the frontrunners moved many lengths clear. Mick's experience told as he took control but Sea The Stars was still boxed in against the rails in the middle of a big pack. John Oxx: 'Mick would not panic as this horse has the gears'. Indeed he had. Deft footwork extricated him as the pack spread out and as they ran to the line he was challenged strongly but simply changed down a gear once again to pull smoothly away from the field to win by two lengths. 'Perfection in equine form – the horse of a lifetime . . .'.

SEA THE STARS — Breeding Pedigree

SEA THE STARS (IRE) b. 2006	**CAPE CROSS** (IRE) b. 1994	**GREEN DESERT** (USA) br. 1983
		PARK APPEAL (IRE) br. 1982
	URBAN SEA (USA) ch. 1989	**MISWAKI** (USA) ch. 1978
		ALLEGRETTA (GB) ch. 1978

DANZIG (USA) dkb/br. 1977	**NORTHERN DANCER** (CAN) b. 1961	**NEARCTIC** (CAN) br. 1954
		NATALMA (USA) b. 1957
	PAS DE NOM (USA) dkb/br. 1968	**ADMIRALS VOYAGE** (USA) dkb/br. 1959
		PETITIONER (GB) b. 1952
FOREIGN COURIER (USA) b. 1979	**SIR IVOR** (USA) b. 1965 [IC]	**SIR GAYLORD** (USA) b. 1959
		ATTICA (USA) ch. 1953
	COURTLY DEE (USA) dkb/br. 1968	**NEVER BEND** (USA) b. 1960
		TULLE (USA) br. 1950
AHONOORA (GB) ch. 1975	**LORENZACCIO** (IRE) ch. 1965	**KLAIRON** (FR) b. 1952
		PHOENISSA (GB) b. 1951
	HELEN NICHOLS (GB) ch. 1966	**MARTIAL** (IRE) ch. 1957
		QUAKER GIRL (GB) gr. 1961
BALIDARESS (IRE) gr. 1973	**BALIDAR** (IRE) br. 1966	**WILL SOMERS** (GB) br. 1955
		VIOLET BANK (GB) b. 1960
	INNOCENCE (GB) gr. 1968	**SEA HAWK** (FR) gr. 1963
		NOVITIATE (GB) ch. 1959
MR PROSPECTOR (USA) b. 1970	**RAISE A NATIVE** (USA) ch. 1961	**NATIVE DANCER** (USA) gr. 1950
		RAISE YOU (USA) ch. 1946
	GOLD DIGGER (USA) b. 1962	**NASHUA** (USA) b. 1952
		SEQUENCE (USA) b. 1946
HOPESPRINGSETERNAL (USA) ch. 1971	**BUCKPASSER** (USA) b. 1963	**TOM FOOL** (USA) b. 1949
		BUSANDA (USA) blk. 1947
	ROSE BOWER (USA) ch. 1958	**PRINCEQUILLO** (IRE) b. 1940
		LEA LANE (USA) b. 1952
LOMBARD (GER) ch. 1967	**AGIO** (GER) b. 1955	**TANTIEME** (FR) b. 1947
		ARALIA (GER) b. 1945
	PROMISED LADY (GB) ch. 1961	**PRINCE CHEVALIER** (FR) b. 1943
		BELLE SAUVAGE (GB) ch. 1949
ANATEVKA (GER) ch. 1969	**ESPRESSO** (GB) ch. 1958	**ACROPOLIS** (GB) ch. 1952
		BABYLON (GB) b. 1940
	ALMYRA (GER) ch. 1962	**BIRKHAHN** (GER) blk/br. 1945
		ALAMEDA (GER) b. 1951

First published in Great Britain in 2009
by Weidenfeld & Nicolson
10 9 8 7 6 5 4 3 2 1

Text © Anne Holland 2009
Design and layout © Weidenfeld & Nicolson 2009

A CIP catalogue record for this book is available
from the British Library.

ISBN: 978 0 297 86076 1
ISBN: 978 0 297 86082 2

Design by www.carrstudio.co.uk
Design assistance by Andrew Campling
Picture research by Caroline Hotblack
Colour reproduction by DL interactive UK
Printed by Printer Trento Srl and bound by L.E.G.O.
SpA, Italy

Weidenfeld & Nicolson
The Orion Publishing Group Ltd
Orion House
5 Upper St Martin's Lane
London WC2H 9EA

An Hachette UK Company

www.orionbooks.co.uk

The Orion Publishing Group's policy is to use
papers that are natural, renewable and recyclable
products and made from wood grown in sustainable
forests. The logging and manufacturing processes
are expected to conform to the environmental
regulations of the country of origin.

Picture Credits

© **Action Images:** 14-15, 21 (bottom), 27 (top), 69
(bottom); © **Colorsport:** 23 (bottom), 24, 25, 28-29,
39, 69 (top); © **Corbis:** 16-17, 18, 19, 34 (top), 37, 38,
72, 139; © **Getty Images:** 20 (bottom), 42-43, 47, 49, 52
(top), 74 (top), 78, 134 (right), 135 (bottom); © **Healy
Racing:** 1, 4, 6-7, 13, 20 (top), 26, 40, 50-51, 53, 60, 63
(top), 68, 73, 76, 79 (all), 80-81, 85 (both), 86 (both),
87, 90-91 (top), 98-99 (top), 101 (bottom), 104-105
(all), 112 (top), 114, 118, 120 (both), 121 (top right),
122-123, 128-129, 132-133 (all), 136-137, 140, 144-145,
148-149, 150, 155, 159; © **Anne Holland:** 34 (bottom);
© **Inpho Photography/ www.inpho.ie:** 9, 10-11, 21 (top),
44, 54, 58-59, 63 (bottom), 64 (both), 65 (bottom),
66-67, 88-89, 91 (bottom), 106, 119, 121 (bottom);
© **Tony Parks / Horse & Hound / IPC+ Syndication:** 2, 3,
8, 12, 41, 82, 138, 147; © **Irish Image Collection/Axiom:**
30, 32-33, 35 (both); © **Peter Mooney:** 77, 121 (top left),
141, 142, 146; © **Photocall Ireland:** 46, 84; © **Racingfotos.
com** 23 (top), 27 (bottom), 70-71, 74 (bottom), 92-93, 94,
97 (both), 98-99 (bottom), 100, 101 (top), 102-103, 107,
108-109, 110, 112 (bottom), 113 (both), 116-117, 126
(bottom), 127 (top), 130, 134 (left), 135 (top); © **John
Reardon:** 22: © **George Selwyn:** 62; © **Sportsfile:** 36, 45,
48, 52 (bottom), 55 (both), 56, 57, 65, (top); © **VCUQ
Qatar/Markus Elblaus:** 126 (top).

Mixed Sources
Product group from well-managed
forests and other controlled sources
www.fsc.org Cert no. CQ-COC-000012
© 1996 Forest Stewardship Council

FSC